Programs and Parties for Christmas

D0932134

Programs and Parties for Christmas

Helen and Larry Eisenberg

BAKER BOOK HOUSE

Grand Rapids, Michigan 49506

ISBN: 0-8010-3359-4

Preface

During Advent we celebrate God's sending of His Son Jesus, the incarnation of His own character and love, to live the life of mortal man. We marvel that God sent a Savior who loves and forgives—and that He came in the form of a baby, born to a humble peasant girl in a stable.

Since its inception Christmas has been a time of festival. Today we celebrate with solemn programs but also with parties, banquets, art, gifts, written communications, hospitality, and other forms of festivity.

It is our hope that this book will be of practical help to you and your co-workers as you plan to celebrate the true joy of Christmas.

Grove, Oklahoma
December 1979

Helen and Larry Eisenberg

Contents

Introduction

How to Use This Book

1. Select someone to head up the entire Advent celebration—the pastor or his wife, the director of Christian ed-
ucation, the Sunday school superintendent, or anyone who is
good at organizing youth or children's programs.

2. Go through the book quickly, underlining and making
notes in the margin when ideas appeal.

3. Let the ideas herein stimulate your own creativity.

4. Take the best ideas to your planning committee. Form
a balanced agenda of Advent-Christmastide programs, parties,
and projects to fit your needs.

5. Having made preliminary plans, re-examine them to
see if you are conveying the real spirit of Christmas.

6. Eventually involve many people in the plans. Don't
try to do all the work by yourself.

Planning for Advent and New Year's Day

The chairperson of the planning committee should present the following questions to the committee on a blackboard, on newsprint, or with an overhead projector. These questions will help shape thinking toward a total approach to the Christmas-Christmastide season which includes New Year's Day.

1. What do we want to achieve? What do we need right now in our families, fellowship, classes, groups, church?

2. What traditions do we want to maintain? Give up?

3. How much time can we spare? How many Sunday mornings, evenings, weeknights, weekdays?

4. What other experiences will our people be having at work, school, in the community? (Be careful not to overload.)

5. What excesses do we want to avoid?

6. What is the balance of activity we need—worship programs, creative experiences, sharing projects, social activities?

7. Shall we call the people to any disciplines of giving, projects, fasting, etc.?

8. What roles do children, youth, and older people play in this celebration? How can we use a lot of people?

9. What shall we create on our own? What shall we borrow from others—programs, scripts, music, banners, decorations, etc.?

10. Shall a New Year celebration be the final focus?

Examining Your Needs

Coming home with his family after a contemporary Christmas celebration, the directing pastor was quite satisfied with the program he had organized. He asked his child how she liked it. She dismissed the issue with *"Where was the baby Jesus?"* And she was right—He hadn't been there.

The church needs to remind itself that Christmas is a celebration of God's great love in the giving of His Son to humanity in a humble stable, surrounded by domestic animals. The original story is utterly awesome, yet simple. We miss Christmas unless we have the childlike spirit of wonder in whatever we do. Christmas is a multi-faceted event.

1. **Scriptural Event.** Ample documentation of the birth of Christ is given in Matthew and Luke for us to compose our very own Christmas program for worship, for a general program, or even as part of a social event.

2. **Gratitude Event.** Our programs will reflect gratefulness, joy, and praise if they are in the spirit of the original humble birth event.

3. **Traditional Event.** Christians of all cultures have their own way of expressing their love of God and their regard for the Christ child. Art, music, drama, and other customs are worth learning about and sharing.

4. **Festival.** Christmas is a time of feasting and lively celebration, both indoors and in the streets. Jesus Himself was frequently seen at social feasting events, and we apparently have His approval.

5. **Family Event.** Through the centuries humanity has been drawn to the Christmas story of the humble little family— loving mother, father, child. God's gift of His Son via the human family is the validation of the family in His plan.

6. **Child-honoring Event.** In Christian circles, Christmas is the universal child festival. Child participation is the heartbeat of Christmas!

Where Can We Have Programs?

Most obvious are worship services for the congregation, worked out with the pastor. Cantatas, Scripture and carol services, dramatics, blends of chancel drama and preaching, and special preaching series are some possibilities. Individual classes and departments of the church can utilize many of the same kinds of activities.

The church can also sponsor Christmas Christian art presentations, caroling, and good will projects both in the church and in the community. These give opportunity for doing loving things for people in Christ's name and for presenting the Christmas story in various ways.

Social events such as parties and banquets are important for promoting Christian fellowship. Christian entertainment will remind people of our reasons for celebration. Social events might be held in homes, at the church, in camp settings, or outdoors.

Themes

The following suggested themes are to be used throughout Advent.

1. **The World's Hungry.** This might involve special projects to raise or collect money to be distributed through church channels or through such organizations as World Vision or CARE. Try having a "meager meal" or "starvation banquet" as explained in the following section on Christmas for Others.

2. **A "Great Music" Christmas.** Choirs sing Christmas Carols, anthems and oratorios, using works from famous composers, e.g. Handel, Bach.

3. **Christmas in the Arts.** Have special displays of paintings and use music and drama extensively.

4. **An Outdoor Christmas.** Feature a live nativity scene or sponsor a family retreat at a camp, perhaps reproducing the Bethlehem scene as part of the program there. Decorate the church property and parsonage in unusual ways.

5. **"Holy Land" Theme.** This is especially appropriate if some members have been to the Holy Land and can help with Christmas programming, banquets, and so on.

6. **Christmas for Others.** Make an effort to find those in the community who are in need of food and fellowship. (See the following section on Christmas for Others.)

7. **What Does Christmas Mean?** Concentrate on the symbolism and customs of Christmas, making or interpreting a chrismon tree, encouraging groups and classes to examine the real meaning of Christmas. Restore use of the manger as the center of Christmas rather than the Christmas tree.

8. **A Creative Christmas.** Encourage creativity in making decorations, writing music, putting together a devotional booklet for Advent, using imagination in programs and services during the season.

9. **Intergenerational Christmas.** Plan programs so that the young, old, and those in between may experience the joyous occasions of Advent together—working, playing, singing, and praying together.

Christmas for Others

1. **Caring for the Lonely.** Visit or send cards to handicapped or elderly persons. For people in nursing homes, present skits, sing carols, or read to them. Remember they need personal attention and affection. Encourage them to participate.

2. **Hotline.** Provide a telephone number to be called by anyone who has a special need during the Advent season, such as transportation, errands, or odd jobs for the elderly.

3. **Help!** Have a committee or person assigned to read the local newspaper, listen to the radio, or watch the television news during the Christmas season, so that you will be aware of and ready to help anyone in special need—those whose homes have burned or who have been in serious accidents, and so on.

4. **Christmas for Prisoners.** Pack bags of fruit and candy along with a Gospel of John or New Testament for inmates in correctional facilities. Your gift may be the only one many receive.

5. **Adoptions.** As a family or church, "adopt" a child, elderly person, or foreign student to share Christmas festivities. This includes meals, presents, and fellowship, depending on the need and appropriateness. Children or the elderly living in institutions may not be able to leave, but may be visited and entertained.

6. **Mother's Day Out.** Plan a day when volunteer workers babysit while mothers Christmas shop.

7. **Firewood Gathering.** The men and young men of the church could spend a Saturday cutting and hauling firewood for those who need it. This is a good way for those who aren't particularly creative to contribute to the church's total Christmas observation.

8. **Playing Santa for Groups.** If your church or individual members own Santa suits, find volunteers to act as Santa for local children's or nursing homes.

9. **White Christmas.** Following a special worship service of thanksgiving for God's gifts, people bring to the altar (or manger) gifts of food, wrapped in white, to be given to the poor.

10. **Telecare.** Form a committee to make daily phone calls to the elderly who want to be checked on.

11. **Food Baskets or Boxes.** Gather canned foods and staples several days before Christmas and box them. Contact welfare or social agencies for names of families who would appreciate the food.

12. **Christmas Dinner at Church.** Prepare Christmas dinner for the poor and for those who would otherwise eat alone.

13. **Christmas Meager Meal or Starvation Banquet.** Serve a light meal, charging for it as if it were a full meal. Send the proceeds to a hunger agency.

14. **Meals on Wheels for Christmas.** Serve a hot Christmas dinner to shut-ins with love and perhaps singing.

15. **Baking Love Loaves.** A warm loaf of bread is a wonderful token of love. As a family or church group, deliver loaves while they are still warm.

Projects in the Church

Here are some ideas to help the church express its oneness as a fellowship of Christian believers at Christmas time.

1. **Devotional Guide.** Perhaps on an intergenerational basis, make and duplicate for the church a devotional guide written by members.

2. **Christmas Edition of the Church Newsletter.** If your church doesn't have a monthly newsletter, make the Christmas issue an annual tradition. Include news of church groups and individuals, inspirational prose and poetry, history, and suggestions for observing Christmas.

3. **Christmas Post Office.** Alphabetize shoe boxes or other containers and set them up in a convenient location for

church members to "mail" their Christmas greetings to one another. Ask them to contribute the money they save on postage to some special Christmas project.

4. **Christmas Resources Table.** Set up an area for selling Bibles, Scripture portions, religious books, art, and jewelry to be purchased as Christmas gifts. Perhaps these materials may be had on a consignment basis from a religious bookstore.

5. **Book Exchange.** During Advent ask members to bring religious or children's books to the church to exchange.

6. **Poinsettia Projects.** Encourage members to bring poinsettias to decorate the church during Advent. Or take poinsettias to the homebound in your community.

7. **Art/Music Festival.** During Advent and Christmastide some churches have displays of great religious paintings as a part of their program. After your annual cantata or Christmas program encourage people to stay to observe the paintings and enjoy refreshments.

8. **Gift Bazaar.** Often used as a money-making project, the Christmas bazaar offers creative, homemade gifts.

9. **Kitchen Presents.** Some organization in your church may want to furnish the church kitchen with food staples, utensils, cookware, or tableware.

10. **Pre-Christmas Services.** Laypersons may want to organize short early-morning worship services followed by coffee and donuts on weekdays during Advent. Assign a different person to lead each service. Invite neighboring churches to participate.

11. **Slave Day.** The church youth may want to raise money for a special Christmas project by offering their services for painting, cleaning, running errands, and so on.

12. **Church Clean-up Day.** Organize volunteers to spend a day between Christmas and New Year's Day taking down

decorations and cleaning the church closets, classrooms, kitchen, and so on. Serve a light lunch for the workers.

13. **Good Deeds for Ministers and Church Staff.** To show love to your church leaders give a gift of time (babysitting, baking, caroling) or purchase a gift. Church workers should also receive public appreciation at Christmas time.

14. **"Pounding" for Your Minister.** "In the olden days" in rural America church members brought a pound of something (sugar, shortening, flour) as a gift for their pastor. Perhaps you could bring your own canned or baked goods. Extend this project to include gifts for other workers.

1

Celebrating Christmas

Christmas Calendar

Date	Observance
November 30	**St. Andrew's Day.** Andrew, disciple of Christ and brother of Peter, is the patron saint of Scotland, Hungary, and Burgundy. Gifts are often exchanged on this day in memory of Andrew's sacrificial death.
December 6	**St. Nicholas Day.** On this day St. Nicholas is supposed to have borrowed the Norse god Odin's reindeer and visited homes, putting sweets in children's shoes on the hearth. Feasting and gift giving are modern-day festivities, especially in northern Europe.
December 13	**St. Lucia's Day.** In the days of the Roman Empire Lucia was tortured for her faith in

Christ. Tradition says that she was dragged behind oxen and finally boiled in oil. St. Lucia's Day is primarily observed in Scandinavia.

December 16 **La Posada.** In Mexico nine days of celebration precede Christmas. People walk through towns depicting Mary and Joseph's journey to Bethlehem. They stop at homes to ask for lodging and are refused, until reaching the designated home where they are received for refreshments and fellowship.

December 24 **Christmas Eve** is celebrated differently throughout the world. In some countries oil lamps are lighted at the appearance of the first star. Candles and yule logs are also lighted. Caroling, feasting, and celebrating of Christ's Mass at midnight are common activities. St. Nick, Santa Claus, or Father Christmas comes, bringing presents for good children.

December 25 **Christmas Day** is most commonly celebrated in the home with feasting and gift giving in commemoration of Christ's birth in Bethlehem.

December 26 **St. Stephen's Day,** also known in England as Boxing Day, is so named because boxes of gifts are brought to the cathedrals and given to the poor.

December 31 **New Year's Eve watch night** services are held at midnight to see the old year out and to bring the new year in with Christian inspiration.

January 6 **The twelfth day of Christmas,** sometimes

called "old Christmas." In Italy St. Befana gives gifts to good children.

Christmas Symbols

Advent wreath. Advent begins on the fourth Sunday before Christmas. Advent wreaths hold four candles—one to be lit on the first Sunday, two the next, and so on. Some families use four red candles, others use a combination of lavender and white. Often a large white "Christ candle" decorates the center of the wreath.

Angels. Awesome in appearance, angels visited shepherds watching their flocks to announce Christ's birth.

Ass, or donkey. Mary traveled to Bethlehem on an ass. It was likely one of the animals in the stable during Christ's birth.

Bells. In many European countries bells mark the beginning of Christmas. In England bells toll before midnight on Christmas Eve to warn Satan of the imminent birth of Jesus. Then at midnight there is triumphant pealing to mark the death of Satan and the birth of the Savior.

Camel. The wise men traveled on camels to bring their gifts of love to the Christ child.

Candles are used to symbolize the light of Christ, the light of the world.

Carols. Originally Christmas caroling involved singing and dancing outside the church because of the undignified manner in which the participants carried on. Today groups of carolers travel from house to house singing of the birth of Christ. Many carols are of folk origin, but some now used in churches were composed by trained lyricists and musicians.

20

Cattle. A legend says that cattle kneel and can speak on Christmas Eve. In several countries cattle get special attention at Christmas because they gave up their manger for the Christ child and warmed Him with their breath.

Christmas tree. Tradition says Martin Luther, coming home from a meeting one night, saw the stars shining through the branches of an evergreen tree. He cut a fir tree, took it into his home, and placed candles on its branches. An old written list of tree decorations included such things as apples, colored paper decorations, gold foil, sweets, wafers, and paper roses.

Another legend says that on the night of Christ's birth all the trees of the forest blossomed and bore fruit for the night.

Crèche. The first Christmas crib or manger scene is credited to St. Francis of Assissi, who felt that Christmas needed to be centered around the simplicity of the original holy night. People brought gifts to the manger and sang carols.

Edelweiss. Because of its white purity and star shape, the edelweiss is the Christmas flower in most parts of Europe.

Father Christmas was at one time the legendary Norse god Odin who drove his reindeer through winter to bring the gifts of spring such as new grain and fruit.

Firecrackers are used in the Orient and in some parts of the United States to herald the birth of Christ and to welcome the new year.

Fireplaces have been the traditional means of entry for Santa Claus, Father Christmas, and Italian Lady Befana.

Gifts. Christ was God's gift to the world. The wise men also brought gifts to the Christ child. We commemorate these events today by giving gifts to friends and family.

Greeting cards. Englishman Joseph Cundall published the first greeting cards in 1844.

Holly and ivy. Because of its attractive red berries, holly has been used decoratively in many countries for hundreds of years. It remains green through the winter, harboring the return of the full power of the sun and spring. Early French and English families hung pieces over their doorways to show that Christ was honored within.

Tradition says that Christ's crown of thorns was made with holly, the berries of which originally were white but turned red with blood.

Manger. The land of Bethlehem in the time of Christ was honeycombed with small caves where cattle were kept. Christ's birth place may have been one of these.

Straw and straw ornaments often are used as Christmas decorations symbolic of the humble manger.

Mince pies. Tradition says that for each mince pie a person eats he will have a good month in the coming year.

Mistletoe. Its white berries represent purity, its green leaves, everlasting life.

A Scandinavian myth tells of the handsome god of light and spring, Baldur, who dreamed that his life was in danger. His mother, Frigga, goddess of love, traveled throughout the world asking everything—earth, air, fire, water—not to hurt her son. But jealous Loki, god of fire, had Baldur killed with a dart made of mistletoe.

The white berries represent Frigga's tears. She decreed that the mistletoe would never again be used as a weapon and that she would place a kiss on anyone who passed under it.

Piñata. Originally a custom mainly in Mexico and Central America, the piñata is now a favorite with children everywhere. A clay or papier-mâché container is filled with candy. Often a piñata is shaped like an animal or a star. It is then hung from the ceiling. Children take turns being blindfolded

NO

and swinging at the piñata with a stick. When a child is successful at breaking the piñata all scramble for its contents.

Poinsettias. In 1836 Dr. Joel R. Poinsett, first minister to Mexico returned from there to South Carolina with some small wild plants which he transplanted in his garden. Through special care and cultivation he developed the poinsettia, our Christmas flower. Its star-like shape and red color give it special significance as a Christmas symbol.

A Mexican legend tells of a poor child who wanted to give a gift to the Virgin Mary but had nothing to give. She pulled some wild flowers and gave them, and as she did they were transfigured into the brilliant red flowers which we call poinsettias.

Reindeer. The role of reindeer during the Christmas season goes back to the legend of the Scandinavian god, Odin, who drove his reindeer through winter into spring, bringing growth of grain and fruit. St. Nicholas borrowed Odin's reindeer once a year on December 6 to distribute gifts to children.

Santa Claus has many counterparts—Father Christmas, Italian Lady Befana, Kris Kringle, Swedish Jul Tomten. The name Santa Claus is a shortening of St. Nicholas, the name Dutch settlers of New York used as they brought him to the United States.

St. Nicholas, the beloved Bishop of Myra, who died on December 6, 345, was revered for his generosity and kindness. Tradition says that once a year he borrowed the god Odin's reindeer to bring gifts to fill the shoes of good children who placed them on the hearth.

Another story tells of a poor man, who because of debts was in danger of having to sell his three daughters. One by one St. Nicholas rescued them with the gift of a gold piece thrown into the house. One version says that he dropped one down the chimney and it landed in a stocking hung by the fireplace.

For this reason we still put a golden orange or tangerine in the toe of Christmas stockings.

Sheep and lambs were in the fields with shepherds while Christ was being born. They have been included in pictures, displays, and live nativity scenes as an essential part of Christmas observances.

Star. The Magi followed the star to where Christ lived after the family left Bethlehem. Some countries use the first star on Christmas Eve as the beginning of Christmas festivities. (Sweden has some interesting customs involving stars. See "Sweden" in the next section.)

Wise men. They came to see Christ on a long journey from the East, which may have taken many months. Their arrival is now celebrated in some countries on January 6 by the giving of gifts.

Yule log. At one time it was believed that the sun stood still for the twelve shortest days of the year. A large yule log was secured to burn for this long and more, helping the sun at its weakest to become stronger. Druids blessed it with ceremony at the winter solstice feast, even decorating it with flowers and anointing it with wine.

It was thought best to use a log from a fruit- or nut-bearing tree—oak, hickory, apple, or other fruit. Ceremonially it was sometimes borne by servants, but with the oldest and youngest (old year and new) walking along.

A traditional prayer at the yule log lighting is "May the fire of this log warm the cold. May the hungry be fed, the weary find rest, and may all enjoy heaven's peace."

Christmas in Other Lands

The following information on holiday customs in other lands may be shared at Christmas programs through dramati-

24

zation. Or type up individual information sheets on each country and pass them out for persons to read aloud during your Christmas gathering.

Austria. On St. Nicholas Day, St. Nicholas parades through the streets in full bishop's regalia.

Czechoslovakia. On December 4 girls place twigs from cherry trees in water. If her twig blossoms before Christmas Eve, tradition says the young lady will marry during the coming year.

Denmark. Musicians climb to the church belfry to "blow the Yule" in four directions, signifying that Christmas comes from the four corners of the earth.

England. Bells toll beginning at 11:00 P.M. to warn Satan, the prince of evil, that the Prince of Peace will soon be born. Then at midnight the bells peal merrily to celebrate the victory of the Christ child over Satan.

Finland and Norway. Sheaves of grain for the birds are tied to tall poles in fields.

France. Many homes have a crèche which the children decorate with laurel, holly, stones, and moss. Children also hang stockings or put out shoes for Father Christmas to fill. And they may fill their wooden shoes with oats for the camels on which the wise men are supposed to be traveling.

Adults burn a yule log throughout the holiday season and give gifts on New Year's Day.

On Christmas Eve a great holiday supper is held after midnight, when church bells call people to church. Each merrymaker lights a Christmas candle, and the supper lasts until morning.

Hungary, Poland, and other European countries. Carolers carry a lighted star, representing the star that the Magi followed.

25

Germany. Caroling and church services are a big part of the German Christmas. Advent wreaths with red candles are used in most homes. Christmas trees are decorated mainly with lights and candy. Presents are distributed on Christmas Eve.

An old German legend says that on Christmas Eve the Virgin Mary and angels visit. Candles are placed in windows to guide them and food is left on the table for them.

Ireland. Long candles are placed in windows to light the way for the Christ child. Only women named Mary are supposed to snuff the candles out on Christmas Day.

Italy. Carolers dress as shepherds and sing from house to house accompanied by bagpipes.

A jewel-crowned figure representing the Christ child lies in the crèche. Legends tell of the healing of people who approached the crèche.

Another Italian legend says that Lady Befana was told by the shepherds of Christ's birth and was urged to go worship Him. But she delayed. Ever since she has wandered in search of the Holy Child, leaving gifts at each house, in hopes that He is within.

Mexico is known for the poinsettia, *flor de Nochebuena*— "flower of Holy Night."

Beginning December 16 the people enact the Posada. Nightly they walk through towns portraying Mary and Joseph's journey to Bethlehem. Joseph knocks on doors, asks for lodging, and is refused.

The crèche is important in Mexico and Latin American countries. Many families have nativity scenes so large that they fill an entire room.

On Christmas Eve children break the piñata. The holy day meal is served late on Christmas Eve.

On January 6, the Feast of Epiphany, balloons of all shapes and colors are enjoyed.

Philippines. A special dish of fruit and sprouts is made and served to all people over age twelve on Christmas Eve. One person stays home to serve guests while others go to share the meal with someone else.

Poland. Children dress as goats, horses, cows, lambs, storks, bears, wolves, or as characters in the nativity. They travel from house to house, singing carols. Gifts of food are given to them.

On Christmas Eve some children are put to bed on straw or hay in imitation of the newborn Christ.

The mass at midnight on Christmas Eve is called the "Mass of the Shepherds."

A Polish proverb says, "A guest in the home is God in the home." A strict fast is held on Christmas Eve until the first star appears, then a feast is served. A chair is left vacant for the holy child.

Russia. A caroling custom has been for a group to pull a beautiful girl on a sled, stopping at each house to carol.

Scotland. Great bonfires are often the center of New Year's Eve celebrations.

Spain. December 8 is the Feast of the Immaculate Conception. Manger scenes called *nacimientos* appear in shops in early December. During the week before Christmas people gather around these and carol. Gifts for children are left by men dressed as the Magi and parades are held to honor the three kings.

Cattle are given special attention during the holidays to commemorate their warming of the manger where Jesus was born.

Sweden. Some Scandinavian customs date back to pre-Christian days. Pagans believed the dead returned to earth on Christmas and they set out food for them. Now children set out food for Santa.

27

December 13 is St. Lucia's Day. A young girl dressed in white with a crown of candles in her hair is followed by other youth carrying burning candles, they awaken sleeping families at dawn and serve them wheat cakes and coffee. This is also observed in individual families.

As in some other countries, the Swedish celebrate the star of Christ's birth with star boys and the three wise men, who go through towns singing, followed by costumed characters.

Switzerland. The Swiss hold that at Christmas time animals speak. Special care is given to animals because they warmed the manger.

Yugoslavia. An interesting custom here is Mother's Day, which comes on the second Sunday before Christmas. While mother sits in her chair, pretending not to notice, a child slips in and ties her feet to the chair. The other children all come in shouting, "Mother's Day, Mother's Day—what will you pay to get away?" She gives them presents and is released. The next Sunday father receives the same treatment.

Prayer in Christmas Planning

Prayer is one of the most appropriate and meaningful Christmas activities. Your planning committee should provide opportunities for church members to pray.

1. **Prayer Partners.** For a month two family members, Sunday school classmates, or church members agree to pray for each other daily and to check with each other for special needs.

2. **Prayer Request Book.** Place on the altar an open notebook where requests can be written. On the opposite page have a sign-up list for those who will pledge to pray for the requests listed.

28

3. **Prayer Breakfast.** The Advent-Christmastide season is a good time to launch a weekly, bi-weekly, or monthly prayer breakfast for men, ladies, teens, or mixed groups.

4. **Prayer with Shut-ins.** Starting December 1 volunteers call on homebound persons each day for conversation and prayer, asking them to pray also.

5. **Prayer Emphasis in Sunday School Classes.** Ask teachers to lead their classes in a special time of prayer during Advent.

6. **Conversational Prayer.** Form groups of three or four and have each person pray for any specific needs. Members of a group pray in natural conversational speech as if the Lord is sitting with them in their group. After about ten minutes of prayer or when the groups are finished, close by praying or singing the Lord's Prayer.

7. **Prayer Vigil.** In preparation for any special services your church may be planning during the Christmas season, you may want to hold a twenty-four-hour prayer vigil in which participants pledge to pray at specific times.

Christmas Music

Music is essential for good Christmas celebration. Many churches will have cantatas, carol singing during services, and house-to-house caroling. Your church can do a bit more.

1. Include the choir director and other musical leaders in the general planning.

2. Besides singing familiar carols, introduce new ones. The choir could help through the four Sundays of Advent. If a tune is unfamiliar, they might sing a stanza and then let the congregation join in. Also, they might sing carols as special numbers, allowing for later use by the congregation.

3. If such an idea as "A Great Day of Singing" is used with music and Scripture during the holiday season, themes such as these might be used:

   a. Sing carols by great composers, such as Handel and Mendelssohn.
   b. Sing carols from different countries.
   c. Dramatize the narrative carols that tell a running story.
   d. Use background information (see following section) to help people understand the song.
   e. Ask the musically talented to compose original carols, perhaps to familiar tunes. Some of the loveliest tunes are in 3/4 or 6/8 time, making guitar accompaniment easy.

4. For caroling, tape accompaniments on guitar, accordian, or other instrument and carry a portable tape recorder.

5. Your choir may want to sing carols on a local radio station.

6. Candlelight caroling services may be held indoors or outdoors. Check with your local fire marshal to see if an indoor candlelight service is safe in your particular facilities.

Scripture, especially the Christmas story, could be interspersed throughout the service.

Follow up the singing with refreshments.

What's Behind the Carol

Did you know that it was once illegal to celebrate Christmas?

In 1644 the English Parliament passed a law banning Christmas celebrations, and not until the beginning of the nineteenth century was the ban lifted and Christmas accepted as a Christian festival.

From long before the birth of Christ pagans celebrated the passing of the sun through its shortest days into the lengthening of days. After Christ came and more and more people became Christian, they disliked giving up the fun of their winter celebration, so they sought to give it Christian meaning.

In England some of our Christmas carols began as rollicking melodies sung by waits, or wandering minstrels, who expected money or food in return. Gradually these songs were fitted with Christian words about the birth, death, and resurrection of Jesus. But still, because of their simple, joyful tunes and because they often were accompanied by dancing, these carols were not thought worthy of use in churches.

Englishman William Sandys (pronounced "Sands") gathered some of these carols and had them published in book form in 1833. This did much to restore Christmas carols to favor. Gradually beautiful poetic carols were written and fitted to more elegant melodies. Today our churches use both the simple and the elegant.

Here we will delve into the history behind some of our favorite carols.

"O Come, O Come Immanuel" may be our oldest Christmas hymn, having been developed from a Latin song of praise used in the twelfth century. The earliest church music was restricted to the singing of the Psalms or portions of them. Later it became allowable to sing antiphons after or responsively with the Psalms. The Seven Greater Antiphons are sung in Anglican churches in England during the Advent season. In the thirteenth century someone took part of these chants and made them into a hymn with a regular rhythm. It was this hymn that Dr. J. M. Neale translated in 1851, and eight years later it found its way into a trial edition of *Hymns Ancient and Modern*.

"Good Christian Men, Rejoice" dates back to the four-teenth century when it began to be acceptable in Germany to mix Latin and German words in church music. Martin Luther in his efforts to reform the Roman Catholic Church encouraged putting German translations into sacred services.

John Mason Neale retranslated the poetry to include it in his book *Carols for Christmastide*, which appeared in 1853.

The melody is thought to be a thirteenth-century tune, which verifies that a good song never dies. It reminds us of pealing bells, rung in regular beat, proclaiming the excitement of the first Christmas.

"What Child Is This?" is sung to the old English mel-ody, "Greensleeves," found in print in 1642 in a book titled *New Christmas Carols*. Its steady rhythm suggests that it was used as a festival dance tune in the days when feasting was interspersed with singing and dancing.

The words were written by William Chatterton Dix, who was a doctor's son in Bristol, England. He was born in 1837 and died in 1898. His vocation was managing an insurance company at Glasgow, Scotland, but his heart was really in writing poetry and devotional literature. He also enjoyed trans-lating hymns into English from Greek and Abyssinian hymn-books. "What Child Is This?" was included in his book *Christmas Customs and Christmas Carols*.

"While Shepherds Watched Their Flocks by Night" dates back at least to 1700 when it first appeared in a supple-ment by Nahum Tate to his earlier book entitled *A New Version of the Psalms Fitted to the Tunes Used in the Churches*. Tate, who was poet-laureate under King William III, collaborated with Chaplain Dr. Nicholas Brady on this. Of the sixteen hymns included in the supplement, this is the only one still in use. Mr. Tate would probably be surprised that almost three hundred years after he wrote it, this Christmas hymn is still being sung, with very few alterations.

The hymn-poem was matched to an adaptation of a melody taken from the opera *Siroe* by George Frederich Handel. Although he composed only three hymns, much of Handel's music has been adapted for church use.

Handel was born at Halle, Prussia, in 1685, the same year that Bach was born. Handel's father was a surgeon in Germany who wanted his son to go into law practice. However, the boy's musical talent was so obvious that he was allowed to be trained by excellent teachers. He was eleven years old, able to play four instruments well, when he was taken to Berlin to perform as a child prodigy. He returned to his home town of Halle when he was seventeen and studied for a year there while serving as organist at the cathedral. When he was eighteen he went to Hamburg, and in three years he wrote four operas. From there he traveled to Italy to study operatic style, writing many compositions in his three years there. In his early twenties he went to England and was immediately well received. He lived there for fifty years. He began composing oratorios when he was fifty-three years old, abandoning the earlier Italian opera style. He is buried in the Poet's Corner of Westminster Abbey in London. Performances of Handel's *Messiah* continue to inspire people of all nations, and "While Shepherds Watched Their Flocks by Night" is one of our favorite songs of Christmas.

"Hark! the Herald Angels Sing," one of the most famous of hymns, was written by Charles Wesley and fitted to music by Felix Mendelssohn-Bartholdy.

After the day in 1738 when Charles Wesley came to the point where he "consciously believed," he became probably the world's most prolific writer of joyful, expressive hymns. He is credited with writing over six thousand songs.

33

Written in 1739, his first two lines of this Christmas hymn were "Hark! how all the welkin rings 'Glory to the King of Kings,' " which is the way it was first published in *Hymns and Sacred Poems*. This was altered by George Whitefield to "Hark! the herald angels sing, 'Glory to the new-born King.' "

Later in 1760 the last two lines also underwent a change. The Reverend Martin Madan changed them from "Universal nature say 'Christ the Lord is risen today,' " to the way we sing it, "With th' angelic hosts proclaim, 'Christ is born in Bethlehem.' "

A few other changes were made before it was added to Tate and Brady's supplement of the *New Version*.

The music of this carol was composed by Ludwig Felix Mendelssohn-Bartholdy when he was thirty-one years old. It was part of an impressive work titled *Festgesang*, but the composer said of it, ". . . it will *never* do to sacred words." However, Dr. William H. Cummings thought otherwise, so in 1855 he set the words of "Hark! the Herald Angels Sing" to this music. Dr. Cummings was principal of the Guildhall School of Music in London.

Felix Mendelssohn was born in 1809 in Hamburg, Germany. His father was a well-to-do banker, who must have been greatly influenced by his garden caretaker named Bartholdy. He wished his children to be brought up as Protestant Christians and he affixed Bartholdy to the name Mendelssohn to indicate that they were no longer of the orthodox Jewish faith. Felix was another child prodigy, giving concerts at the age of ten and composing songs by age twelve. He was a dynamic and tireless composer and traveler, and he did much to restore the music of Bach to public attention.

"Silent Night" was written as a poem by Joseph Mohr in 1818, to be given as a Christmas gift to his friend, the schoolmaster and church organist Franz Gruber. Joseph Mohr was born in 1792 in Salzburg, Austria. He became a Roman Catholic priest in 1815, and for thirty-three years served churches near his hometown.

When Mr. Gruber received this lovely poem, he immediately set to work to compose a melody to fit it. The same evening he and some of his friends, with guitar accompaniment, sang it at a Christmas celebration in the Arnsdorf schoolhouse. The words and music were so simple and beautiful that it quickly spread across Germany and Austria. In America, we find it first in the *Sunday School Hymnal* in 1871. It has become a favorite of all ages.

"It Came Upon the Midnight Clear" is an American hymn written in 1849 by Edmund Hamilton Sears. At that time it was titled "Peace on Earth," which seems to have been a favorite theme of American hymnwriters. Twenty years later it was included in a British book of hymns.

Edmund H. Sears was born in Massachusetts in 1810 and was educated at Union College and Harvard Divinity School. He became a Unitarian preacher, but made it plain that though he "was educated in the Unitarian denomination" he believed and preached "the divinity of Christ." Most of his ministry was in Wayland, Massachusetts, where he preached and wrote hymns.

We don't know if Richard Storrs Willis knew Mr. Sears, but it is quite likely that he did. The same year that this hymn was printed, 1850, Mr. Willis composed the music to go with it. He had gone to Yale University, studied also in Germany, and then taught German to Yale students. Later he edited the *Musical Times*. He also wrote a biography of his friend Mendelssohn, whom he had met in Germany. He died in Detroit in 1900.

"**Joy to the World**" is a paraphrase of the second half of Psalm 98, and it has come down to us with only one word changed since it appeared in the 1719 edition of *Psalms of David Imitated in the Language of the New Testament* written by Isaac Watts.

Who was this Isaac Watts who in an age of strict traditionalism dared to paraphrase Holy Scripture? Perhaps his nonconformity sprang from his mother's side of the family. Her ancestors were Huguenots, the Protestants in a Catholic-dominated France who were persecuted and massacred for their faith. Or perhaps it was his father's influence. Enoch Watts was twice imprisoned in England for his Puritan beliefs. Mrs. Watts would take Isaac, her firstborn of nine children, to the prison gates where she would bravely encourage her husband and others by singing psalms. When the father was out of prison he served as deacon in the Congregational church in Southampton, England. Once the young Isaac complained to his father about the dullness of the singing. He was told to write something better if he could. This was a great challenge to him. His first hymn, "Behold the Glories of the Lamb" had this message: "Prepare *new* honours for His name, And songs before unknown." The congregation accepted this hymn gladly, so he continued to supply them with a new hymn each Sunday for two years. And throughout his lifetime Dr. Watts wrote many theological, philosophical, and poetic works.

The music of this Christmas hymn, "Joy to the World," is taken here and there from among portions of Handel's *Messiah*, and many early sources give him the credit. However, other arrangers have added and subtracted until it is difficult to know exactly who should get the credit. The tune or variations of it have been named "Comfort," "Antioch," "Jerusalem," "Holy Triumph," and "Messiah."

36

Christmas Decorations

Your group may wish to have a pre-Hanging-of-the-Greens party to collect or make a variety of decorations before the first Sunday in Advent. Encourage families to make decorations together.

Here are a few decorating suggestions.

1. **Greens.** Gather greens, pine cones, berries, and weeds in advance. Some have to be dried. Evergreens dipped in starch hold imitation snow.

2. **Christmas Cards.** Use old Christmas cards for tree ornaments or table decorations.

3. **Fireplace.** If you don't have one, make one by tacking brick or fireplace paper over boxes.

4. **Snowman.** Perhaps a youth class would like to make one by covering two bushel baskets with white cloth, stuffing an old pillow case for the head, and inking in features such as eyes, nose, clothing, etc. Or use construction paper cutouts for features.

5. **Snowflakes.** With a compass make a circle in the center of a square white piece of paper. Mark off six points and fold on these points so that a scissors design can be made on all sides with one cut. Use your imagination. Attach snowflakes to windows, mirrors, or walls with cellophane tape or hang them from the ceiling.

6. **Toothpick balls** are made by sticking round toothpicks into a soft, round cork or styrofoam ball. Spray paint them and then sprinkle with glitter.

7. **Giant Christmas cards** can be made from posterboard and used as decorations or as gifts for special persons.

8. **Angel Choir.** Decorate mantles, shelves, or tables with angel figures made from gumdrops, toothpicks, peppermints, and construction paper.

9. **Luminarios.** A decorating custom of Mexican origin is to fill the bottoms of paper bags (size 8 or larger) with sand, roll the tops down, and burn large candles in them. Used in quantity these make a lovely way to line the walks to churches or homes after dark.

Planning Your Hanging of the Greens

1. Pre-plan what decorations will go where, considering the church yard and outside of the building, inside walls, halls, rooms, windows, and so on. Perhaps each class will want to decorate its own room.

If you have professional decorators in your church, make use of their services.

Provide equipment such as ladders, hammers, scissors, tape, glue, tacks, etc.

Decorations for the tree, wreaths, candles, and so on can be made at home or by shut-ins ahead of time. (See the following pages for ideas.)

2. Appoint one or more roving directors to move from room to room during the decorating to give creative help.

3. Gather greens in advance. Girls and women enjoy a hike in the woods as much as the men and boys do. Store fresh greens in a cool moist place to keep them from drying and fading.

4. Also in advance have a committee look through old decorations to see what condition they are in. Check electrical decorations, such as lights, for wiring defects and replace burnt-out bulbs.

5. If a special tree is to be prepared for the feeding of birds, bring the necessary food and supplies.

6. If Christmas music is to be broadcast from the church tower, make sure someone is in charge and that equipment is in working order.

7. Include children. The Hanging of the Greens is one of the best opportunities your church will have for multi-generational participation.

8. Poinsettia Project. Order small poinsettias for homebound church members. Use them as decorations one week, then distribute them.

9. Large cut-out letters of an appropriate saying such as, "For unto us a child is born" or "For God so loved He gave" may be hung in your church fellowship hall.

10. Christmas quotations lettered with felt pens on posterboard may be placed throughout the church. This is a good youth project.

11. Have a committee serve coffee, hot chocolate, and cold drinks during the decorating activities. The kitchen committee may also provide colored popcorn for decorating, bake cookies, or sponsor a taffy pull.

12. Schedule dismantling. During the hanging of the greens announce plans for taking the decorations down and packing them away. Have a sign-up sheet for specific duties.

Christmas Tree Ideas

1. **Old tree/new tree.** If your church has two trees, decorate one with old-fashioned ornaments, and strings of popcorn and cranberries. Decorate the other tree with chrismons.

2. **Whimsical trees.** Make trees out of fruit, pop cans, balloons (form shell out of coat hangers), Christmas cards, and so on. Or decorate an evergreen with icicles made of pop can pulls or straws.

3. **Sweet decorations.** Wrap nuts, candies, and cookies in cellophane. Make chains by taping the sweets together.

4. **Decorate the base** of your tree with popcorn (to look like snow), cones, magnolia leaves, and presents.

5. **Snowflakes** (see preceding section on Christmas Decorations for instructions).

6. **Bird tree.** After Christmas mount your used evergreen outside and hang bread, suet, seeds, and fruit on it. Children especially enjoy this project.

Chrismons for the Christmas Tree

Services in which a Christmas tree is decorated with white and gold symbols relating to Christ have become very popular. These symbols are called *chrismons*, a contraction of the words *Christ monograms*. A Lutheran laywoman from Danville, Virginia, is credited with this idea.

Various groups, classes, or individuals are requested to prepare one or more symbols of similar size to be hung on a Christmas tree, accompanied by an explanation of the meaning it has. Symbols originally were called *monograms*—signs which mean "Jesus." These may be made of thin white styrofoam and edged or decorated with gold glitter. (Some have been cut from the lids of white egg cartons.) A few examples are given here, with descriptions that may be used to explain them as they are hung on the tree.

The first Christians were often persecuted by people who did not understand or appreciate their faith in Christ. Therefore it was necessary for Christians to have symbols to identify themselves to each other, but which would be obscure to non-Christians.

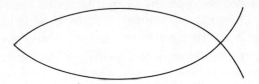

Fish

One of the earliest signs used was the fish. This was especially appropriate because the Greek word for fish is *ichthus*. Since "I" was the first letter in the Greek spelling of *Jesus*, "Ch" was the beginning of the word *Christ*, "Th" was the start of the Greek word for *God*, "U" began the word *Son*, and "S" stood for the word *Savior*, *ichthus* was an acrostic, spelling the first letters of "Jesus Christ, Son of God, Savior."

This symbol could easily be drawn by two casual sweeps of the sandal in the road, identifying to Christians where a worship meeting would be held. Some ancient drawings found on Christian tombs show a fish carrying a basket of bread loaves and a pitcher of wine, a reminder of Jesus' last supper.

Lamb

The lamb as a symbol for Christ can be traced to the prophecies of Isaiah in the Old Testament. He prophesied that

41

there would come upon the earth a Man who would take away the sins of mankind by offering Himself as a lamb for the slaughter. It was the custom in ancient Hebrew days for everyone to go to Jerusalem once a year for a Passover celebration, held in memory of the time when in Egypt the Jewish children were saved from death by painting lamb's blood on their doorposts, as God had commanded them through Moses. During the Passover each family brought the temple priests a lamb to be offered as a sacrifice to God as a form of thankful expression for His protection, and as a repentance offering for their sins.

When Jesus came to the Jordan River to be baptized by John the Baptist, his second cousin, John cried out to the onlookers, "Behold, the Lamb of God, who takes away the sins of the world."

The lamb is a good symbol for Jesus. A lamb is gentle and obedient to his shepherd. Jesus said, "I came to do the will of my Father."

In the writings of John which we call the Revelation, a vision was described of a large book sealed with seven seals.

42

The Lamb was the only being worthy of opening the seals. Another symbol has grown from this Scripture—a book clamped shut by seven seals, with a lamb lying on top of it.

Sometimes a lamb is pictured as marching with a banner on which there is a cross. The staff from which the banner floats is also shaped like a cross. In this symbol, the lamb has his head thrown up as a sign of victory because of resurrection. A cloud surrounds the lamb's head, with rays of light penetrating the cloud from three directions. Many tombs of early Christians have drawings of lambs on them.

Shepherd

The shepherd is another way Jesus described Himself, adding, "The good shepherd lays down his life for the sheep." In many church windows, Jesus is depicted as a shepherd holding a lamb. He once told His disciples that if a shepherd had a hundred sheep and one got lost, he would leave the ninety-nine in the sheepfold to go hunt for the lost one. He was indicating God's love for any person who strays.

If a sheep fell into a crevice, the shepherd would use his long staff to lift him up. The shepherd's staff has also become a symbol of Jesus.

43

Crown

Frequently a sparkling white and gold crown is used to top the chrismon tree. The Suffering Servant is in this way declared to be King or Lord of all. Royalty was a status earthly kings and queens achieved at birth, but maintaining this position depended on the loyalty and obedience of their subjects.

Jesus' claim to the throne of our hearts existed before He was born, based on who He was, is, and ever will be. Anyone may become part of His kingdom by making Him king of his life, giving Him love, reverence, and obedience.

Chi-Rho

The oldest monogram for Jesus Christ is the Chi-Rho. It looks like a cross drawn over the stem of the letter "P"; the "P" being the Greek letter rho, and the "X" being called chi.

When used together they form the first two letters in the word *Christ*. This monogram is frequently used on the pulpit and lectern cloths. The first royal convert to Christianity was the Roman emperor Constantine the First, who lived from A.D.

272-337. He had the Chi-Rho painted on his soldiers' banners and shields after seeing a vision one night of this symbol in the sky, and with it in Latin the words, "In this sign thou shalt conquer." He did win the battle, and eventually ruled the entire Western Empire. He then ordered all persecution of Christians to be stopped.

Crosses

Some books say that the emblem seen in the sky by Constantine was a cross. Truly the cross has come to symbolize the death of Jesus. In some churches the figure of Christ is shown on the cross, while in others the cross is shown empty to acknowledge Christ's resurrection. Many cross designs have developed in Christian art; however, the simple Latin cross is the one used most.

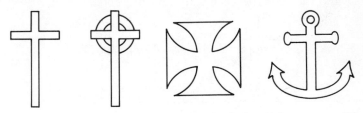

In many cemeteries one can find the Celtic cross. This has a circle around the intersection of the cross pieces. The circle stands for eternal or everlasting life.

The Maltese cross was developed as the emblem for the Knights of Saint John, a group of laymen in the eleventh century, organized to protect pilgrims to the Holy Land from being attacked by thieves and murderers. They had their headquarters on the island of Malta. This cross flares like a trumpet at the end of each crosspiece.

One of the oldest forms of the cross is called the anchor cross, developed in the early days of persecution. To the uninformed, it looks merely like an anchor, but a Christian could spot the cross incorporated into its design. In many places the Lord is called "our hope," and in Hebrews 6:19, this hope is described as a sure and steadfast anchor of the soul.

Many early Christians used the anchor as their tomb decoration, a declaration that even in death their hope was for an eternal kingdom with Christ as King.

Alpha-Omega

The two Greek letters, alpha and omega are excellent monograms for *Jesus*. The alpha looks just like our capital letter "A" while the omega looks more like an inverted "U." When these two letters are shown with a symbol for Christ, it becomes a reference to Revelation 22:13, where Christ is declared "the first and the last, the beginning and the end."

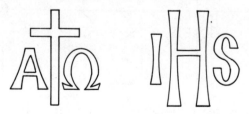

Frequently we see the monogram "IHS" engraved on crosses or altars. This is an adapted form of the first three letters of the Greek word for *Jesus* (ΙΚΣΟΥΣ). The third letter, the sigma, which looks like "M" lying on its left side, eventually fell out of use and an "S" was substituted. Both monograms are still in use, an abbreviation for *Jesus*.

INRI

Often we see the monogram "INRI" on a cross. These are the first letters for the inscription Pilate ordered placed atop Jesus' cross: *Iesus Nazarenus Rex Iudaeorum*. This was done in Greek, Latin, and Hebrew. The Jews wanted the sign changed to "He says he is King of the Jews," but Pilate refused to change it. In English we would read, "Jesus of Nazareth, King of the Jews."

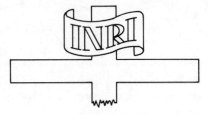

Stars

The five-pointed star is called the Star of Bethlehem or the Star of Epiphany commemorating the journey of the wise men of the East to see Jesus. The season of Epiphany continues for twelve days after Christmas and is to be a time of rededication to spreading the good news of Jesus.

47

A six-pointed star symbolizes God as Father. The Jews call it the Star of David. Each point reminds us of the characteristics of God: power, wisdom, majesty, love, mercy, justice.

Holy Spirit

The Holy Spirit is represented by a star with seven points, each point symbolizing one of the gifts the Spirit bestows— power, riches, wisdom, strength, honor, glory, and blessing.

The twelve-pointed star represents the twelve tribes of Israel or the twelve apostles of Jesus.

Other symbols relating to Jesus may be found, such as the candle symbolizing Christ's statement, "I am the light of the world," the descending dove of the Holy Spirit which came down from heaven upon Jesus at the time of His baptism, the trefoil and overlapping three circles indicating the threefold nature of the Trinity—God the Father, God the Son, God the Holy Spirit.

Preparing the styrofoam and glitter decorations may include a thorough study of religious symbols. When the decorations are complete with gold cord inserted for hanging, they may be hung on a tree decorated with gold garlands. If lights are used, they should be white or clear.

Having a chrismon tree may become an annual tradition. What a good way to put Christ back into Christmas!

Christmas Windows

1. **Wrapping paper windows.** Sketch a design for a stained-glass window on a small piece of paper, then enlarge it and cut it out of wrapping paper. Sketch in the design with chalk or pencil, and paint in the leading around the panes with black paint. Use crayons or acrylic paints to fill in the design. Apply linseed oil on the back of the picture and wipe off the excess to allow the light to shine through.

2. **Cellophane windows.** Paint your design on clear cellophane, using black India ink or show-card color for the leading. Or attach colored cellophane figures to clear cellophane with tape.

3. **Tissue paper windows.** Glue your design on black tissue paper.

4. **Art glass windows.** Using a nativity scene as your subject, it is possible to work out several ideas:

a. A blue silhouette pasted to the window.
b. India ink and watercolor "art glass" on architect's drafting paper.
c. Aluminum foil silhouette with a blue spotlight behind.

Candle-Making

Items needed: paraffin, containers for melting paraffin, bowls for beating paraffin, molds, egg beaters, forks, spatula, skewer to melt holes for wicks, crayons, oil paints, or purchased candle coloring such as Vivi-Tone.

Wicks. Prepare wicks of heavy cotton yarn, twisted cotton trout line, or something similar by soaking them overnight in a solution of two tablespoons Borax and a tablespoon of salt in a cup of water.

Heat the wax over a low flame or over hot water. Caution: wax can explode or catch on fire. If this happens cover the wax with lid of container to smother flames.

Color the wax by melting crayons, oil colors, or Vivi-Tone in hot wax. A half-inch crayon will color a quart-sized candle. (Save enough colored wax to reheat and fill the pit which forms in the center of the candle when it cools.)

Molding. Fill pint, quart, or half-gallon milk cartons, potato chip containers, oatmeal boxes, tin cans, tin jello molds, glass jars, or fancy-shaped vases (remembering that glass containers must be removed—broken off—when the wax hardens). See that there are no creases or rough edges to keep the candle from releasing from the mold when hardened. Let cool thoroughly before inserting the wick.

Drill a hole or insert a hot skewer to create a hole and put in the wick, which has been stiffened with a coat of wax.

Frosting the candle. Melt wax, pour the mixture into a

bowl, and let it set until a film forms around the edge of the bowl. Beat with an egg beater—faster motion produces fluffy frosting, similar to the consistency of whipping cream. Apply with fork, leaving open spaces for glow effect, beginning at the bottom and working toward the top. The frosting may be tinted with a brush after the candle has been frosted. (Whipping makes colored wax lighter in color.)

Uses of wax art. Many varieties of candles can be made: large illuminating candles, snowball candles in graduated sizes, molded star design table centerpieces, floating candles, nut cups, candle snowmen, and so on. Use your imagination.

Molded candles. Snowballs, hearts, stars, bells, and so on may be made by molding the two halves in bowls or jello molds. Melt the flat edges of the two molds and stick them together. The wick may be inserted when the molds are put together or it may be put in later.

Decorating the candles. Paste on stickers and use candle rings to brighten up your candles. Or make figures to stick on the candles by melting wax and forming a thin layer in a shallow pan. While the wax is soft and pliable, cut out designs, then shape them with your fingers. Stick the designs—leaves, petals, flowers, etc.—on the candle with melted wax.

2

Program Ideas

Christmas Program Idea Starters

Let these program ideas spark your creativity.

1. **Christmas and Chanukah.** If you live in a community where there are a number of Jews, you may want to invite a Jew to explain to your church the background and customs of Chanukah.

2. **The Symbolism of Christmas.** (See section on chrismons.) Make chrismons and plan an entire program around hanging them on a tree with oral presentations of their meanings. Have the choir sing carols between hanging of symbols. You may want a speech choir to present the information that goes with the symbols. Be sure to rehearse.

3. **"Great Day of Singing."** Have the choir, special groups, soloists, and the congregation sing Christmas music. Intersperse with Scripture reading and testimonies.

4. **Legend of the Christ Child.** Write one-act plays based on the legend that on Christmas Eve the Christ child wanders the earth, seeking food and shelter. Use the Golden Rule as your theme.

5. **The Holy Spirit and Christmas.** As you read the Christmas story in Matthew and Luke, you may be impressed with the number of times the Holy Spirit is mentioned. Trace the Holy Spirit's activity in skits or in an oral presentation.

6. **Light Shine.** Isaiah foresaw Jesus as the Light of the World. Write a play or program using Isaiah as the narrator (see Isa. 9, etc.) and weave in the New Testament story.

7. **At the Bethlehem Inn.** Write a play or interview based on the reactions of the innkeeper, his wife, servants, and guests at the Bethlehem inn on the night of Christ's birth.

8. **The Christmas People.** Write a program telling about each person in the Christmas story: Elizabeth, Zacharias, John, Joseph, Mary, Jesus, shepherds, Simeon, Anna, Herod, the wise men. Sing carols between oral presentations.

9. **The Lord Is My Shepherd.** Write a program based on Psalm 23 but reflecting the Christmas story by using mainly Matthew's and Luke's accounts. Emphasize that Christ was sent for each one of us to be our Shepherd.

10. **Tell Me the Stories of Jesus.** Have people pose in frozen scenes (use special lighting effects) to depict different portions of Jesus' life. Use music and Scripture reading—perhaps a speech choir—to tell the stories of Jesus.

11. **Yes, Virginia, There Is a Santa Claus!** Using Virginia O'Hanlon's letter to the *New York Sun*, have a speaker pick up on the points made by the *Sun's* editorial writer.

12. **Bobby's Christmas Star.** Write a children's play about Bobby, a little boy who heard about and wanted to find the Christmas star. He did several good deeds for people in his

neighborhood, and afterwards many of these people told Bobby that they saw the star.

13. **Christmas Gift.** Write a youth play about a basketball player or cheerleader who was "done wrong" by someone but forgave at Christmas time.

14. **Live Crèche.** Present a live nativity for a number of evenings before Christmas, acting out the scene two or three times each night. Taking care of the animals will be the biggest responsibility.

Advent Candle Lighting

The Advent wreath is usually fifteen inches or so in diameter, containing four candles, with a "Christ candle" in the center. Often a child and an adult will participate in the lighting, with the child lighting the candle and the adult reading or expounding on a passage of Scripture. Here are some possibilities.

First Sunday: Read Isaiah 9:1-7 or concentrate on Isaiah 9:2, emphasizing the hope of the light Jesus brought to mankind as the Messiah. After the message ask the child to light the candle. Then have the choir, a group, or all sing a stanza of "O Come, O Come, Immanuel."

Second Sunday. Read Luke 2:1-7, or emphasize verses 6 and 7. "Last Sunday we lit one candle, symbolizing Jesus as the Light of the World. Today we present the stable, warm in spite of its humble setting. . . ." Light two candles. Ask the children to sing, "Away in a Manger."

Third Sunday. Read Luke 2:8-20, emphasizing verse 20. "Today we relight the two candles of our first two Sundays in Advent, representing light and warmth, and we will light a third to represent joy." Tell the story and focus on the surprise and joy of the shepherds, both in the fields and in the discovery of the Christ child in Bethlehem. With the lighting of the three candles, all or a group might sing "Joy to the World."

Fourth Sunday. Read Matthew 2:1-12, directing attention to verses 1-2. Review what the other three candles represent—light, warmth, and joy. The fourth symbolizes the guiding star, the star of Christ. Sing the chorus of "We Three Kings." Following this could be a service with the theme, "Wise Men Still Follow the Star."

Some Portraits of Jesus

This program uses carols and Scripture to describe some of the names Jesus was called. We suggest using two readers for voice contrast.

Reader 1: Welcome to our program! Today we will look at the many names that Christians have called Jesus.

Reader 2: Genesis tells us that "in the beginning God created." The Gospel of John, calling Jesus the "Word" says, "In the beginning was the Word, and the Word was with God, and the Word was God."

Reader 1: Another great name for Jesus is "Immanuel." Let's sing "O Come, O Come, Immanuel." Immanuel means, "God with us." (Sing.) Other great names for Jesus in that hymn are "Wisdom from on high," "Desire of nations," and "Dayspring."

The Jews had for hundreds of years expected the coming of the Messiah, the Anointed One. Isaiah 9:6 tells us more names for the promised Messiah: "For unto us a child is born, unto us a son is given:

and the government shall be upon his shoulder: and his name shall be called Wonderful Counsellor, the mighty God, the everlasting Father, the Prince of Peace." Handel's *Messiah* tells us of this. But let us now turn to a Christmas carol that explains in its words the hopes of the people for a Messiah: "Come, Thou Long-expected Jesus."

Reader 2: In Zechariah 9:9 we find Jesus called King, Righteous One, and Victor, yet humbly riding on a donkey's colt. The lovely French carol, "Angels We Have Heard on High," tells the story of His birth. Our choir will sing the verses and all of us will join them singing the "Gloria in Excelsis Deo" refrain.

Reader 1: Son of God and Love's Pure Light are two more terms we use for the Master. First, let us sing the three stanzas of "Silent Night," then I will read the love chapter, I Corinthians 13.

Reader 2: King of Kings is another of those glorious titles we give to Jesus the Christ. Enjoy the singing of "What Child Is This?" by our singers.

Reader 1: Christians believe that Jesus was sent to earth on a special mission of God to deliver us from our sins. Therefore He is also called Deliverer. The carol "O Little Town of Bethlehem" tells the Christmas story and also points this out, calling Jesus "Holy Child of Bethlehem." Before we sing this carol I would like to read the words while you close your eyes and meditate on them. (Read.) Now let's sing these stanzas.

Reader 2: Ours is a skeptical age; many doubt the existence of angels in the Christmas story. But we know that the shepherds were convinced that they heard the angels sing. Now the choir will sing "Hark! the Herald Angels Sing!" When they reach the part that says "Glory to the newborn king," join in as if you were the angels. This phrase is found twice in the first stanza.

Reader 1:   The carol we just sang also calls Jesus, "second Adam." We might say that the first Adam got mankind into trouble and the second Adam delivers us from it!

As we sing this last hymn think of the title *Lord*. Christians are to take Jesus as Savior and Lord. Somehow we seem happier to have Him deliver us from our troubles than to be Lord of our lives! *Lord* means "total director." It means that we must be humble enough to submit, to give Him first place in our hearts. Let us stand and sing "Joy to the World."

Reader 2:   We hope you have enjoyed this experience of music and Scripture! We now ask the pastor to give the benediction.

Note: This format can be modified, expanded, using different words, carols, and Scripture, and perhaps using more of the Christmas story in Scripture. Choir, soloists, and ensembles might also be used.

Remembering Jesus

Narrator: Tonight (today) our setting is the upper room. The followers of Jesus, including the twelve disciples, are here in faithfulness to His command in Luke 24:49: ". . . but tarry ye in the city of Jerusalem, until ye be endued with power from on high." The 120 have been here for some days now, praying and praising God. Now they are reminiscing. First we hear the apostle Peter.

Peter: Mary, how did you feel when the angel told you that you would be the Messiah's mother?

Mary: At first I could not believe that I, a simple young girl, could be chosen as the mother of our Lord.

Peter: Tell us, Mary, what do you remember of Him most?

Mary: I remember how sensitive and loving He was. When His half-brothers and I couldn't understand Him, He still loved us and was so patient with us.

And I remember the night He was born. How tired I was, but oh, how proud. He was such a beautiful baby! Even the animals seemed to know that something unusual was happening. The innkeeper gave us some warm things and when Jesus was born, I wrapped Him in swaddling clothes. From the very first He was such a loving child. But you twelve must remember some things about Him that I never experienced. What were they?

Narrator: Here the disciples begin to reminisce.

Disciple 1: I'll tell you what I remember about the Master. Some people once brought their children to Him to be blessed and prayed for. We didn't know then how much He loved children, so we said, "You must not bother Him."

	But He said, "Let the little children come to me. Don't prevent them, for of such is the kingdom of heaven!"
Narrator:	We read that today in Matthew 19:14. Listen, another disciple is speaking.
Disciple 2:	Let me tell you a story I remember that He told. It is about a man who was going from Jerusalem to Jericho and was beaten by robbers. A priest and a temple assistant passed the man by, but Jesus told us that a Samaritan took care of the man's wounds, took him to an inn, paid for his care, and said, "If it costs more, I will pay you later." Jesus told us this to show us what it means to be a neighbor. He said that our neighbor is anyone in need.
Narrator:	And that is preserved for us in Luke 10:29. Now here is another disciple.
Disciple 3:	Yes, that reminds me of what He told us about the last judgment. He will be the King and will judge all people. He said that the righteous were the sheep and evil ones, the goats. The Master said that He would say, "Come, you blessed, into the kingdom . . . for I was hungry and you fed me; thirsty and you gave me water; I was a stranger and you took me home; naked and you clothed me; sick and in prison and you visited me." Then He told us that the righteous would ask when they had done all this and He would say, "When you do it to my brothers, you do it to me."
Narrator:	And that is the spirit of Jesus that has carried

over into Christmas through many years. Now another disciple is remembering.

Disciple 4: I remember what He said about being born again. We didn't have any idea what that meant at the time. He taught us that men can only reproduce human life, but that He could give us new life. Then He taught us that the Father loved us so much that He gave the Master to die, so that any of us who believe on Him should not perish but have everlasting life with Him.

Narrator: When the disciples were remembering, these things had not yet been written down. We know now that He is speaking of John 3:16. Here is another disciple.

Disciple 5: Dear friends and brothers, many things I remember, but one I remember especially clearly: "Do for others what you want them to do to you."

Disciple 6: Yes, and He taught us the commandment of love. He said that the greatest was, "Hear, O Israel! The Lord our God is the one and only God." Then He said, "And you must love Him with all your heart and soul and mind and strength." And right after that, He said, "The second is, 'You must love others as much as yourself.' " He said that there are no commandments greater than these.

Narrator: Perhaps when Jesus said these things, His disciples did not fully realize how important they were, especially this last commandment. Now another disciple speaks up.

Disciple 7: We didn't know what He was saying at the time,

but right after He told us He was to die for us, He said, "If anyone wants to be a real follower of mine, let him deny himself, take up his cross and follow me. For anyone who keeps his life for himself shall lose it, and anyone who loses his life for me shall find it again." I am only beginning to understand what He means.

Disciple 8: Well, I remember when we were in Gethsemane with Him and just couldn't stay awake while He prayed. He said, "Be alert and pray, or temptation will overpower you. For the spirit is willing but the flesh is weak."

Narrator: Isn't it great that Matthew records this for us in chapter 26, verse 41? Now the disciples continue to talk about Jesus.

Disciple 9: The most beautiful thing I remember about the Master happened at the cross. He looked at the ones who were taunting Him and brutally crucifying Him and said with such love, "Father, forgive these people, for they don't know what they are doing."

Disciple 10: Do you remember the day when He was teaching us about heaven? He said, "There are many homes where my Father lives, and I am going to prepare a place for your coming." I didn't know it then, but I know now how little we deserve that love of His, the way we deserted Him. But I will never forget His love when He came back to us after His resurrection from the dead. He loved each one of us personally.

Narrator: Yes, and it is just as hard today to realize that

61

even though we don't deserve His love, He loves each one of us. Love is the story of Jesus, from the manger in Bethlehem to the resurrection.

Disciple 11: During the passover meal when He was with us for the last time, I shall never forget what He did in taking the bread and wine. He told us how much He had counted on eating this meal with us. Right after Judas had dipped his bread in the dish, Jesus broke the bread and gave it to us and said, "Take it and eat it, for it is my body. . . ." And then He took the cup and said, "Each one of you drink from it, for this is my blood of the new covenant. It is poured out for the sins of multitudes." Then He gave it to us.

Disciple 12: My most treasured memory is when we were in the mountains of Galilee. Just before He left us He said, "I have been given full authority in heaven and earth. Go and make disciples of all nations, baptizing them in the name of the Father, and of the Son, and of the Holy Spirit. Teach these new disciples to obey all the commandments I have given you. And be sure of this: I will be with you always, even to the end of the world."

Narrator: Not only did His disciples remember these things. Today we too remember them and they give comfort and direction to us. Soon after this experience in the upper room, the 120 were filled with the Holy Spirit and power, so much so that when Peter preached, three thousand people were added to the church.

No less than then, Christ today calls for disciples, and makes to them the same promises and lays on them the same claims. We give you a moment of silent meditation to reflect on your own discipleship.

Let us pledge our discipleship to Him as we sing ——————.

A Christian Festival of Lights

This colorful festival may be presented where people are seated around tables or from a central stage or altar. It will be most effective in a setting where all will be in darkness except for a spotlighted manger scene or imitation stained glass window high on a wall. Flashlights may be used for spotlighting. If some low lighting seems necessary, use candles in colored glass containers tall enough to hide the bright glow of the flame, but casting a pleasant glow of color here and there.

You will need an assortment of candles of varying colors and lengths, placed along one side of a long table or altar with a person behind each candle. A tall slender taper of white should be in the center. As each candle is lighted, an excerpt from the Bible is read aloud. The progression will be from each end of the table, alternating until the final taper in the center is lighted. Two blue tapers in low candle holders or with collars to catch the drips will be handed from the outermost speakers to those next in line as each reader (or speaker) completes his or her particular reading.

If necessary, one reader may read all the Scripture references, while two candle-lighters pass slowly from the outer candles to the center, pausing for each reading.

Reader 1:   In the beginning God created the heaven and the earth. And the earth was without form, and void; and darkness was upon the face of the deep. And the Spirit of God moved upon the face of the waters. And God said, Let there be light: and there was light (Gen. 1:1-3).

Reader 2:   I will raise them up a Prophet from among their brethren, like unto thee, and will put my words in his mouth; and he shall speak unto them all that I shall command him (Deut. 18:18).

Reader 3:   Out of the mouths of babes and sucklings hast thou ordained strength because of thine enemies, that thou mightest still the enemy and the avenger. When I consider thy heavens, the work of thy fingers, the moon and the stars, which thou hast ordained; What is man, that thou art mindful of him? and the son of man, that thou visitest him? (Ps. 8:2-4).

Reader 4:   Blessed be he that cometh in the name of the Lord: we have blessed you out of the house of the Lord. God is the Lord, which hath shewed us light (Ps. 118:26-27a).

Reader 5:   Therefore the Lord himself shall give you a sign; Behold, a virgin shall conceive, and bear a son, and shall call his name Immanuel (Isa. 7:14).

Reader 6:   The people that walked in darkness have seen a great light: they that dwell in the land of the shadow of death, upon them hath the light shined. For unto us a child is born, unto us a son is given: and the government shall be upon his shoulder: and his name shall be called Wonderful Counsellor, The mighty God, The everlasting Father, The Prince of Peace (Isa. 9:2, 6).

Reader 7: And he said, It is a light thing that thou shouldest be my servant to raise up the tribes of Jacob, and to restore the preserved of Israel: I will also give thee for a light to the Gentiles, that thou mayest be my salvation unto the end of the earth (Isa. 49:6).

Reader 8: But thou, Bethlehem Ephratah, though thou be little among the thousands of Judah, yet out of thee shall he come forth unto me that is to be ruler in Israel; whose goings forth have been from of old, from everlasting (Mic. 5:2).

Reader 9: And in the sixth month the angel Gabriel was sent from God unto a city of Galilee, named Nazareth, to a virgin espoused to a man whose name was Joseph, of the house of David; and the virgin's name was Mary. And the angel came in unto her, and said, Hail, thou that art highly favoured, the Lord is with thee; blessed art thou among women (Luke 1:26-28).

Reader 10: And the angel said unto her, Fear not, Mary: for thou hast found favour with God. And, behold, thou shalt conceive in thy womb, and bring forth a son, and shalt call his name Jesus. He shall be great, and shall be called the Son of the Highest: and the Lord God shall give unto him the throne of his father David: And he shall reign over the house of Jacob for ever; and of his kingdom there shall be no end (Luke 1:30-33).

Center
Candle-
lighter:

(Take both blue tapers, using one to light the tall white taper in the center, then hold both blue tapers while reciting.) And Joseph also went up from Galilee, out of the city of Nazareth, into Judea, unto the city of David, which is called Bethlehem (because he was of the house and lineage of David); to be taxed with Mary his espoused wife, being great with child. And so it was, that, while they were there, the days were accomplished that she should be delivered. And she brought forth her firstborn son, and wrapped him in swaddling clothes, and laid him in a manger; because there was no room for them in the inn. And there were in the same country shepherds abiding in the field, keeping watch over their flock by night. And, lo, the angel of the Lord came upon them, and the glory of the Lord shone round about them: and they were sore afraid. And the angel said unto them, Fear not: for, behold, I bring you good tidings of great joy, which shall be to all people. For unto you is born this day in the city of David a Saviour, which is Christ the Lord. And this shall be a sign unto you; Ye shall find the babe wrapped in swaddling clothes, lying in a manger. And suddenly there was with the angel a multitude of the heavenly host praising God, and saying, Glory to God in the highest, and on earth peace, good will toward men (Luke 2:4-14).

66

Conclude by singing "Joy to the World." If, however, the ceremony is held in a church sanctuary, having the choir sing "Hallelujah!" from Handel's *Messiah* would be a triumphant conclusion.

If the program needs to be extended, hymns referring to the given Scripture portions might be sung after each recitation.

Following Reader 1, we suggest the first stanza of "How Great Thou Art" or the first two stanzas of "O Day of Rest and Gladness."

After Reader 2 choose a hymn such as "Join All the Glorious Names"—first two stanzas, "O Come, O Come, Immanuel," or "We've a Story to Tell."

Following Reader 3 sing "I Wonder As I Wander" or "Redeeming Love."

Reader 4 may be followed by singing "The Light of the World Is Jesus," "Blessed Be the Name," or "O How Glorious, Full of Wonder."

Following Reader 5 sing "Hark! The Herald Angels Sing" or "Lo!, How a Rose E'er Blooming."

After Reader 6 sing "He Shall Be Called Wonderful" or "The People That in Darkness Sat."

Following Reader 7 sing "We, Thy People, Praise Thee" or "The Light of the World Is Jesus."

"O Little Town of Bethlehem" or "O Come All Ye Faithful" would make a good emphasis following Reader 8.

Reader 9 could be followed by the first stanza of "Have Thine Own Way, Lord" or "Breathe on Me, Breath of God."

After Reader 10 sing "Come, Thou Long-expected Jesus" or "Child in the Manger."

As mentioned earlier, after the recitation given by the center candle-lighter, "Joy to the World" would make a happy finale.

It is hoped that this festival of lights will be used in many homes, encouraging the memorization of the ancient prophecies and the fulfillment in the birth of Christ as recorded in the New Testament. To encourage its use, churches may wish to mimeograph the program for family use.

Born the King of Angels

This program may be used at a banquet or as a worship service. If used at a banquet, ask the banqueters to bring angel centerpieces. You will see all kinds—ceramic, metal, fabric and feathers, wood, styrofoam and net, paper, and papier-mâché. Candles and greenery should be provided.

On the back of the banquet program print these questions as conversation starters.

1. What are the names of two angels mentioned in the Bible?
2. Do all angels have wings? How many do seraphim have?
3. Give one example of when an animal saw an angel before a person did.
4. Mary, mother of Jesus, saw and talked with an angel. Did Joseph?
5. When Daniel fasted and prayed, an angel came to him. Who was that angel?
6. Do children have guardian angels?
7. Describe a time mentioned in Scripture when angels looked like men.

The program is divided into two parts. Part One is concerned with angels mentioned in the four Gospels and their activity in the life of Jesus. Two readers with contrasting voices should be used. We have designated them "M" for masculine and "F" for feminine.

Part Two is based on information in both the Old and New Testaments concerning the appearance and ministry of angels. It ends with the question, "Are angels still involved with humankind?" In Part Two various bits of information are typed up on nine slips of paper and are passed out before the program to people with strong voices.

Intersperse carols between readings to lengthen program.

Part One

F: Just as the ringing of bells seems especially appropriate for Christmas time, so does the use of angels as part of our season's decor. Indeed, angels play a very important part in the Matthew and Luke accounts of Jesus' conception and birth. First, as if to set the stage for the miraculous coming of the Messiah, an angel appeared to the priest Zacharias as he burned incense to God in the temple. While he was in the Holy Place alone, the congregation remained in deep prayer outside.

M: And there appeared unto him an angel of the Lord standing on the right side of the altar of incense. And when Zacharias saw him, he was troubled, and fear fell upon him. But the angel said unto him, "Fear not, Zacharias: for thy prayer is heard; and thy wife Elisabeth shall bear thee a son, and thou shalt call his name John. . . . And many of the children of Israel shall he turn to the Lord their God. And he shall go before him in the spirit and power of Elias, to turn the hearts of the fathers to the children, and the disobedient to the wisdom of the just; to make ready a people prepared for the Lord."

F: Since both Zacharias and his wife Elisabeth were getting old, Zacharias must have had some doubts, for he asked the angel, "Whereby shall I know this?"

69

M: And the angel answering said unto him, "I am Gabriel, that stand in the presence of God; and am sent to speak unto thee, and to shew thee these glad tidings. And, behold, thou shalt be dumb, and not able to speak, until the day that these things shall be performed, because thou believest not my words, which shall be fulfilled in their season."

F: In Elisabeth's sixth month of pregnancy the angel Gabriel was sent from God unto a city of Galilee, named Nazareth, to a virgin espoused to a man whose name was Joseph, of the house of David; and the virgin's name was Mary. And the angel came in unto her and said,

M: "Hail, thou that art highly favoured, the Lord is with thee: blessed art thou among women."

F: As we can well understand, Mary was trying intently to understand what the angel meant by this greeting. So the angel said unto her:

M: "Fear not, Mary: for thou hast found favour with God. And, behold, thou shalt conceive in thy womb, and bring forth a son, and shalt call his name JESUS. He shall be great, and shall be called the Son of the Highest: and the Lord God shall give unto him the throne of his father David: And he shall reign over the house of Jacob for ever; and of his kingdom there shall be no end."

F: Then Mary said to the angel, "How shall this be, seeing I know not a man?"

M: The reply given was that the Holy Ghost would come upon her and the power of the Highest would overshadow her. Then, as if to prove his reliability, the angel told her about her cousin Elisabeth's pregnancy, reminding her that "with God nothing shall be impossible." Mary obviously believed this word, for her response was:

F: "Behold the handmaid of the Lord; be it unto me according to thy word."

M: The angel Gabriel, as we have heard from these Scriptures, spoke directly to Zacharias and Mary. However, the man to whom Mary was espoused had yet to be informed, and we are told that while he was pondering how to privately break his engagement to Mary, an angel appeared to him in a dream, saying:

F: "Joseph, thou son of David, fear not to take unto thee Mary thy wife: for that which is conceived in her is of the Holy Ghost. And she shall bring forth a son, and thou shalt call his name JESUS: for he shall save his people from their sins."

M: So Joseph did not hesitate to take Mary for his wife.

F: Meanwhile, back in the hill country of Judaea, Elisabeth's son was born and Zacharias was given back his ability to speak. He promptly began praising the Lord, and the word quickly spread that God was doing something special. According to Luke's account, the reaction of the hill people was that of fear, but they laid up in their hearts what was being said and wondered, "What manner of child shall this be?" About this time the Holy Spirit filled Zacharias, causing him to bring forth praise to God and this prophecy about John:

M: ". . . And thou, child, shalt be called the prophet of the Highest: for thou shalt go before the face of the Lord to prepare his ways; to give knowledge of salvation unto his people by the remission of their sins, through the tender mercy of our God; whereby the dayspring from on high hath visited us."

F: The days passed, and the time for Mary to give birth

71

coincided with the time that Joseph and Mary were required to journey to Bethlehem to pay their taxes. As we know, the inn had already filled, so Jesus was born in the stable. Again an angel appeared, this time to some shepherds guarding their sheep in the fields at night. It is recorded that the angel of the Lord came upon them, and the glory of the Lord shone round about them. Naturally, they were afraid. But the angel said:

M: "Fear not: for behold, I bring you good tidings of great joy, which shall be to all people. For unto you is born this day in the city of David a Saviour, which is Christ the Lord. And this shall be a sign unto you: ye shall find the babe wrapped in swaddling clothes, lying in a manger."

F: After announcing this, the angel was joined by a multitude of other angels praising God, and saying,

M: "Glory to God in the highest, and on earth peace, good will toward men."

F: These angels returned to heaven. Then Matthew reports that wise men from the east—we might call them astrologers—came seeking the babe, bringing expensive gifts. They inquired at Herod's palace of the whereabouts of the new King of the Jews, and Herod craftily told them that when they located Him, supposedly in Bethlehem, they must let him know so he could come to worship Him also. The wise men, however, were warned in a dream that they should not return to Herod. About this time an angel appeared to Joseph in a dream saying to him:

M: "Arise, and take the young child and his mother, and flee into Egypt, and be thou there until I bring thee word: for Herod will seek the young child to destroy him."

F: Matthew records that Joseph, Mary, and the young child Jesus fled immediately by night into Egypt and remained there until Joseph, after being informed by an angel in a dream that Herod had died, returned with them to Israel. Again, however, Joseph was warned by God in a dream, and he turned aside into parts of Galilee, finally settling in Nazareth. We have no further recorded accounts of angelic visitations with relation to Jesus until after He was baptized by His second cousin John, son of Zacharias, and was promptly led by the Holy Spirit into a forty-day fast in the wilderness of Judaea. During those days of physical and spiritual testing the fallen angel, Satan, came to tempt Jesus. After victoriously overcoming Satan's suggestions by quoting Scripture, Jesus was ministered to by angels.

       Holy angels are not mentioned again until Jesus' time of prayer in Gethsemane, when after asking His disciples repeatedly to watch and pray, only to have them go to sleep, an angel came and strengthened Him.

       Matthew's account of Jesus' resurrection is most graphic. He wrote that a great earthquake came at that time, and the angel of the Lord descended from heaven, and came and rolled back the stone from the door, and sat upon it. His countenance was like lightning, and his raiment white as snow: and for fear of him the keepers did shake and became as dead men. And the angel answered and said unto the women,

M: "Fear not ye: for I know that ye seek Jesus, which was crucified. He is not here: for he is risen, as he said. Come and see the place where the Lord lay. And go quickly and tell his disciples that he is risen from the dead; and

73

behold, he goeth before you into Galilee; there shall ye see him: lo, I have told you."

F: Mark describes the resurrection morning this way: the three Marys (one also called Salome) brought spices to anoint Jesus' body and were wondering how to get the huge stone rolled away from the tomb entrance. They were surprised to find it already rolled away. So they entered the sepulchre and saw a young man sitting on the right side, clothed in a long white garment; and they were afraid. This young man then told them not to be afraid, but to go tell Jesus' disciples that they would see Him later in Galilee.

M: Luke describes the resurrection this way: Early on that resurrection morning several women brought spices to the sepulchre, found the stone rolled away, entered, and saw that Jesus was not there. As they stood perplexed, two men in shining garments appeared. The women bowed down in fear, and the two men spoke to them, reminding them of Jesus' prophecies concerning his crucifixion and resurrection.

F: John states that Mary Magdalene came alone to the grave, and when she saw the stone taken away, she ran to tell Simon Peter and "the other disciple, whom Jesus loved." These two ran to the tomb, saw the abandoned grave clothes and then went home. Mary Magdalene stayed there weeping, and then as she looked again into the tomb she beheld two "angels in white, sitting the one at the head, and the other at the feet, where the body of Jesus had lain."

(Both readers may now be seated unless one of them is to serve as the commentator in Part Two.)

74

Part Two

(The commentator will now call the nine readers to join him and will ask them to read their parts as he calls their numbers.)

C: When we read about angels in Scripture or sing about them in hymns, are we engaging in a bit of poetic fantasy, or do we really believe in angels? If we say we do indeed believe in angels, what do we believe about them? To help us in this consideration, we have gleaned information from several sources, and we hope you will look up some of these for yourselves. We are indebted to Alfred Edersheim's classic, *The Life and Times of Jesus the Messiah*, reprinted recently by William B. Eerdmans Publishing Company; Billy Graham's *Angels*; Mrs. George C. Needham's paperback, *Angels and Demons*, published by Moody Press; *All About Angels* by C. Leslie Miller, Regal Books Division of G/L Publications; and A. C. Gaebelein's *What the Bible Says About Angels*, reissued in 1975 in paperback by Baker Book House.

1:   Nearly three hundred places in the Bible tell us that God has countless angels at His command and that He commissions these angels to aid His children. In the Book of Hebrews we are told that even now the angels are "all ministering spirits, sent forth to minister for them who shall be heirs of salvation."

2:   God has given angels the job of helping with material affairs. When Hagar was fainting in the desert, her son Ishmael about to die, an angel showed her a fountain of water. When Joshua was in a hard situation, an angel with a sword appeared as the Lord's captain. When Peter was in prison, an angel released him. Jesus was fed by angels, defended by angels, and strengthened by angels.

75

3: History hints at graded authority among angels, yet only two names are mentioned in the Bible—Michael and Gabriel. Some ancient rabbinical writings, written after the Hebrews' exile in Babylon, name six or seven. Michael is titled an archangel; we do not hear of other archangels in Scripture except for Lucifer who was renamed Satan after he challenged the position of Almighty God and was cast out of heaven. Apparently Michael has great strength in fighting, for when the messenger angel Gabriel was having difficulty getting to Daniel because of the opposition of the so-called Prince of Persia, Michael came to aid Gabriel in getting past.

4: Another distinct order of angels is the seraphim. Isaiah, in chapter 6, describes them as having six wings. They were above God's throne singing in responsive chant, "Holy, holy, holy, is the Lord of hosts!" In John's Revelation, angels sing, "Worthy is the Lamb," and they minister before the altar with incense.

5: The cherubim, another order of angels, appear to be higher than ordinary angels. When Adam and Eve were sent from Eden, the cherubim were commanded to guard the tree of life. Ezekiel describes them as having wings and hands, but also being full of eyes and surrounded by wheels within wheels. Figures of cherubim were molded into part of the design of the ark of the covenant and woven into the temple draperies.

6: Angels are usually invisible, but at many times they have suddenly become visible—as to Balaam, and as the heavenly hosts suddenly appeared to shepherds near Bethlehem on the night of Christ's birth. Jacob met two hosts of angels, and Moses saw the Lord descend onto Mount Sinai followed by ten thousands of angels. Daniel and

John beheld myriads of angels in heaven. Hebrews mentions "an innumerable company of angels." David writes about twenty thousand chariots and many thousands of angels. And our Lord Jesus said in the garden, "Thinkest thou that I cannot beseech my Father and He shall even now send me more than twelve legions of angels?" (Twelve Roman legions would number 72,000.)

7: Frequently angels are mentioned as messengers of punishment; they use wind, fire, and plagues. The nation and cities of Israel are reported to be under angelic guardianship with Michael as their great prince. When Sennacherib defied God's armies, an angel of the Lord in a single night caused 180,000 Assyrians to die from a hot, smothering wind. When Herod, a Jew with Roman leanings, assumed the honor due divinity, an angel immediately smote him with parasites, causing his death.

8: Sometimes angels appear as ordinary men, as to Lot at Sodom and Gomorrah, and we are advised to be hospitable to strangers because we may be entertaining angels unawares.

9: It is indicated in Scripture that angels carry the holy dead to the part of Paradise where they will rest, as described in the parable about the rich man and Lazarus, and also from the dying words of Stephen. They are to accompany Christ at His second coming, when they will gather the elect from the four corners of the earth.

C: What the Bible records is of the past or the future. What about the now? Are there evidences that angels are even now at work in our world? Whose voice called out to Peter Marshall as he crossed a dark moor one night, thereby saving him from stepping into a deep quarry. Who were the hundreds of big men in shining garments with drawn swords who protected the John Paton couple, missionaries to the New Hebrides, when hostile men came one night to kill them? Who provided the seagull which lighted on Eddie Rickenbacker's head when afloat in the Pacific with six men without food? There are many such accounts which seem unexplainable in any way other than divine intervention.

3

Christmas Programs and Projects for Children

Music

1. **Children's choir.** If your church has a children's choir, use it frequently during the holiday season.

2. **Children's caroling.** Adults, especially senior citizens, enjoy having children sing for them. Check with local nursing homes to see if they will permit children to sing for their patients.

3. **Rhythm Band.** Many popular Christmas tunes have rhythms that children can keep time to with wood blocks, drums, tambourines, bells, and so on.

4. **Parent-child Performances.** Encourage families to sing specials together during the holidays.

Christmas Tree

1. Allow the children's department or individual classes to decorate their own tree.

2. Encourage the children to help the adults decorate the "big tree."

3. Children can make ornaments and paper chains or pop can tab chains and can string popcorn and cranberries.

4. Allow children to help bake and decorate cookies for tree ornaments.

5. Prepare an outdoor tree for the birds.

6. Using risers, have the children form the shape of a Christmas tree, each holding a flashlight with colored tissue paper over the lens as an ornament. Direct them in singing carols. This project can be done indoors or outdoors.

Things to Make

1. Have children decorate cans and fill them with coins during Advent. Then have a special ceremony where the children leave their banks under a Christmas tree or at a manger. Make the children aware of what their money will be used for.

2. Make drawings of the nativity for a bulletin board.

3. Make a Christmas mural on paper tablecloth material or freezer wrap for an empty wall or hallway.

4. Make Christmas cards for the elderly, missionaries, friends, or relatives. Use old Christmas cards, magazine pictures, crayons, construction paper, etc.

Other Activities

1. Ask children to help prepare and deliver baskets of fruit for the elderly.

2. As a Christmas gift for their parents have children make cards with pledges to make beds, help with dishes, care for pets, or other chores.

3. Guide the children in adopting an elderly person as a grandparent during the Christmas season. The children can give their adopted grandparents presents and sing for them. The children could also adopt a needy family or a child in an institution.

4. Plan a time when the children can act out the Christmas story for their classmates. Have them choose their roles and bring their own costumes. Let them tell the story in their own words.

5. If you have a church library encourage the children to check out Christmas books, records, and tapes.

6. Work with the junior high class to prepare a Christmas puppet show for the children.

7. Take children to a farm to see and have contact with types of animals that were at the manger during Christ's birth.

8. Before Christmas have children draw names for exchanging inexpensive gifts, then have a party to pass them out. Be sure to have extra gifts on hand.

4

Christmas Banquets and Parties

Banquets

1. **Progressive Meal.** Using several homes within driving distance of each other, have the crowd (broken up into car-sized groups) go from one home to another on a schedule. One course of the meal is served at each home. Play games, tell stories, and sing for entertainment.

2. **Rustic Banquet.** Make the setting for your banquet somewhat like a stable. Use picnic tables, cover the floor with hay. This is a good idea for a camp or retreat. Plan a program of carols, Scriptures, stories, the nativity, plays, and so on.

3. **International Banquet.** Plan your program using international food, customs, and carols. Perhaps you can show a film or slides of other countries or have a guest speaker who is from or has visited other countries.

4. **Old Fashioned Banquet.** Place someone who is familiar with Christmas traditions of yesteryear in charge of your banquet.

5. **Great Music Banquet.** During and after eating feature the great music of Christmas.

6. **Fruit Basket Banquet.** Number all places at each table. After each course, every person must shift (taking tableware with him) to the next designated location. For instance, if places are numbered one through six, person number one must rotate clockwise to the next number one position, giving him a new set of table partners.

7. **Holy Land Banquet.** If possible have someone who has visited or studied the Holy Land help plan this banquet. Serve Jewish food and afterwards show a film or slides of the Holy Land, present Jewish music, and display any souvenirs available. The meal could be reminiscent of what Mary and Joseph may have eaten. You may want to call this a Bethlehem Banquet.

Planning a Party

A party should be a highly enjoyable experience for all present, with the activities suited to the guests, the place, and the occasion. Here are some elements of a good party:

1. Be sure of a lively beginning by planning mixers to get everyone acquinted and involved.

2. Background music or singing adds cheer to any party, but especially at Christmas time.

3. Play creative group games or contests.

4. Alternate mental games with physical games or skits, building the party to a climax just before refreshments are served.

5. Skits or charades help break the shell around even the shyest of guests.

6. Prepare tasty new refreshments.

7. Close with singing or a devotional service, drawing all guests together.

Party Themes

1. **Caroling.** Any or all age groups can plan a caroling party.

2. **Christmas Card Party.** People of any age group can get together to make cards or decorations or to make tape recordings for friends that are far away.

3. **Christmas Coffee House.** Youth and college students especially enjoy a coffee house setting. Decorate with checked tablecloths and candles in bottles. Have volunteer waiters dress in matching uniforms. Plan a program of music, poetry, Scripture, movies, and slides. Leave time between entertainment segments for guests to socialize, but do have a definite program.

4. **Christmas Picnic.** Invite all ages to an indoor Christmas picnic. Play picnic games and close with a candlelight service. This party is especially nice if held in a room with a fireplace.

5. **Penny Walk.** Have guests meet at the church. There they divide into groups of about four. Each group has a leader who possesses a penny. All walk to the nearest intersection, and upon arrival there the leaders toss their pennies. Heads go to the right, tails to the left. This procedure is followed at each intersection. Combine caroling with the penny walk. Return to the church for games and refreshments.

6. **Possum Hunt.** Cardboard possums are hidden in trees before the party. Clues are written up and distributed, and

guests, equipped with flashlights, divide into small groups to hunt for the possums. Put a time limit on the hunt and have guests return to the church for food and fellowship.

7. **Treasure Hunt.** This is similar to the possum hunt.

8. **Travel Party.** Take your guests to many lands by sharing foreign Christmas customs, songs, stories, dances, souvenirs, and foods. Plan a slide show or movie.

9. **White Elephant Party.** Ask guests to bring white elephants as gifts.

10. **Box Packing Party.** Pack food, fruit, candy, or presents for the poor or for prisoners. (Check with prison authorities to see what gifts are permitted.)

11. **Toy Patching Party.** Collect and repair used toys for needy children. From local welfare agencies get names of those who would appreciate the toys.

12. **Rehearsal Party.** After practicing music or drama for special Christmas services have games and refreshments.

13. **Block Party.** Christmas time is a good time for neighbors to get acquainted. Plan a covered dish meal or have desserts for refreshments.

14. **Salt Shaker Party.** To introduce new people to long-time church members, have a potluck dinner party for four or more couples. Play games or sing for entertainment.

15. **Adoptee Party.** Often at Christmas time classes "adopt" someone in a nursing home, children's home, or prison. Plan a party with your adoptee, including games, singing, and gift giving. If you can't meet with your adoptee, prepare cards, gifts, or a tape recording for him.

16. **Youth Lock-In or Slumber Party.** Have the youth bring sleeping bags and gear for spending a night at the church. Allow them to prepare their own food. For entertainment play games, make cards or decorations, sing, show a movie, or have a devotional time. Be sure to have plenty of chaperones.

17. **Bowl Game Party.** Gather football fans of all ages to watch the football bowl games together. Prepare plenty of snack food.

18. **Bowl Game Widows Party.** Invite the women left alone during the football games for a social time at home or church. Perhaps this would be a good time to clean the church.

19. **Christmas Hobby Show.** Before Christmas invite craft enthusiasts to display and show how to make Christmas crafts. Follow up the presentations with refreshments.

5

Party Materials

Group Starters

1. **Name Tags.** If your guests are new to one another distribute name tags in the form of stars, Christmas trees, Santas, or something else seasonal.

2. **Guess.** Have your guests guess the length of a piece of gift-wrapping ribbon, the number of seeds in three apples displayed, the number of apples in a basket (to be used for refreshments), the number of beans in a jar, or something else.

3. **Mystery Present.** Ask your guests to guess what is in your special box. The person who guesses correctly (or comes close) wins the gift.

4. **Doodles.** As guests sit or stand facing a blackboard, one person takes chalk and makes any kind of line (straight, wavy, curved) on the board. The next person must complete the picture by making something seasonal and recognizable.

After the group has seen it, he erases his picture and starts another doodle.

5. **Pin the Star on the Tree.** Everyone has played Pin the Tail on the Donkey. Blindfold early comers and let them try this version.

Games for Party Fun

These are suitable for home or church, Christmas or any time!

1. **Pass It On.** Seat no more than twenty-five players in a circle. Form two or more circles if necessary. In each circle a wrapped Christmas present is passed as fast as possible while music plays. The object is not to be caught holding the gift when the music stops. When a person is caught, the next time the gift passes him he must pass it under his left leg before passing it on. If he is caught twice he must pass it under his left leg and around his neck before passing it on. The third time he passes it under his left leg, around his neck, and under his right leg. The fourth time he does all these motions and stands up. The fifth time he is caught he does the first four motions, sits back down, and passes the gift on.

2. **The Prophetic Bottle.** Seat no more than twenty-five people in a circle. Put a glass pop bottle in the center, ask it a question, then spin it. For example, "Who is the best looking person here?" "Who is going to get a _____ for Christmas?"

Choose a "bottle sighter," someone of unimpeachable integrity, to sight down the bottle to see whom it is pointing at. The person the bottle points to asks the next question.

3. **Clap Out Rhythm.** Divide the crowd into small groups, perhaps by birth months—January to March, April to June,

and so on. Each group chooses a leader and then works out the rhythm of a Christmas song by clapping. "Jingle Bells" is a give away. When all groups are ready ask them, one at a time, to clap out their song while the others try to guess what it is.

4. **Shouting Proverbs.** Break up into small groups, each with a leader. Ask them to think of proverbs such as "Silence is golden," "Out of sight, out of mind," "All that glitters is not gold," "A stitch in time saves nine."

When the groups have chosen their proverbs the leaders assign one word of their proverb to each player. Then each group is given a turn to perform. The leader says, "One, two, three, word!" and on "word" the players shout their words. All others are to guess the hidden proverb. This game can also be played with song titles.

5. **Human Checkers.** Arrange six players (three males, three females) on seven chairs as shown:

F	F	F	Vacant	M	M	M
1	2	3	Chair	4	5	6

The object of the game is to reverse the order of the checkers by moves and jumps. If you have a large crowd at your party get two or more games going and see who can finish first.

Solution: F3 moves right into the vacant chair. M4 jumps left. M5 moves left. F3 jumps to right. F2 jumps M4. F1 moves right. M4 jumps F1. M5 jumps F2. M6 jumps F3. F3 moves right one place. F3 jumps M6. F1 jumps M5. M5 moves left. M6 jumps F1. F1 moves right.

6. **Shock.** Children love this game. Send a volunteer from the room. When he is gone the leader helps the group select some metallic object in the room. Then the volunteer is called back in and is told that he will be notified by all the

players as soon as he touches the chosen object. He begins touching metal objects such as rings, glasses, hinges, screws, and so on. When he touches the chosen object the group lets out a terrifying scream. The next volunteer knows what to expect but doesn't know when it will happen.

7. **Shoe Scramble.** Ask guests to remove their shoes and place them in a pile in the middle of the room. Scramble the shoes. On signal everyone retrieves his shoes. The first one to put them on wins.

8. **Aunt Sally Went Christmas Shopping.** Each player must act out use of the items Aunt Sally bought as the leader calls the items off. As items are added the players act out use of all at the same time. Here are some suggestions:

1. Electric milker (milking motion)
2. Bubble gum (add chewing motion)
3. A new bicycle (add pedaling motion)
4. A spring seat for the bike (add bouncing motion)
5. A cuckoo clock (Say, "Cuckoo, cuckoo")
6. A spinning wheel (add rocking motion)

9. **Count to Thirty.** First, with your group seated in a circle, practice rhythmically counting to thirty.

Next, explain that instead of saying the word *seven* (including seventeen and twenty-seven) each person will make a seven sign by placing the palms of his hands together.

Then explain that instead of saying the multiples of seven (fourteen, twenty-one, and twenty-eight) each person will make a sign by placing his hands back to back, the middle knuckles of the fingers intersecting at right angles. Practice these first two steps before going on.

Finally, tell the group that each time a sign is used, the direction of the counting is reversed. For example, if the seven sign is used when the counting is clockwise, the direction immediately reverses to counterclockwise. Choose someone to start, ask players to say their numbers loudly, and you are ready to play. Start over when a mistake is made.

10. **Chain Reaction.** This game is similar to Gossip. Three persons are sent from the room. The others plan an act that uses a succession of motions, such as driving, discovering a flat tire, stopping car, getting out, taking out spare tire and tools, and changing tire. One person is chosen to act out the skit.

One at a time the players are called back in. The skit is acted out for number one who in turn acts it out for number two, and number two acts out what he sees for number three. Number three then gives his interpretation of the skit. Finally the group tells the three what the pantomime was intended to be.

11. **Back to Back** (Vis-à-Vis). When the leader calls, "Back to back," guests must find a partner to stand back to back with. Then the leader calls, "Face to face," and the players turn. Next the leader says, "Shake hands ＿＿＿＿＿ style." Here are some examples:

1. Pump handle (pumping action)
2. Model-T Ford (cranking action)
3. Fisherman (motion of a wriggling fish)
4. Paul Bunyan. Begin with a regular handshake then grab your thumb with your free hand and make a sawing motion. Yell, "Timber!" when your tree is cut down.
5. Milkmaid. One person interlaces the fingers of both hands, thumbs down. The other person grasps thumbs and "milks."

Intersperse other orders such as "Knee to knee," "Thumb to thumb," "Nose to nose," and "Side to side" with handshakes.

12. **Camouflage.** Hide ten items in plain view by using camouflage. For example, put a penny on a brown window sill, a folded dollar in a plant, a ring on the tip of the screw that holds a lamp shade in place, a red comb on a red sofa. Divide players into pairs and give each pair a list of items not to be picked up or spoken about. Allow them fifteen to twenty minutes to find and record the whereabouts of each item.

13. **Right or Wrong Quiz.** Players cluster in the middle of a room which has one side marked "right" and the other side marked "wrong." As the leader reads quiz questions the players designate their answers by going to one side of the room or the other. A sample question is, "Camels can go for weeks without water—right or wrong?" The answer is "wrong"; camels can go for about five days without water.

Use questions about Christmas if desired. This game can be adapted for use by teams.

14. **Christmas Indians.** While the guests are casually sitting around, five or more "Indians," "reindeer," "football players," or other characters dressed nearly alike, come charging single file through a doorway then out again. Then they return in different order and the guests must try to arrange them in their original order. This can be done as a team effort.

15. **Scissors Race.** Give each contestant a strip of paper ten feet long. On signal players cut from one end of their strip to the other. First one to finish wins. Use adding machine tape or strips of tablecloth paper. Children will need blunt scissors.

16. **Spoon Photography.** This trick is set up ahead of time by a leader and his partner. The leader will send his partner out of the room and as he leaves the leader will imitate the pose of someone in the room. Then the partner will reenter the room and the leader will say, "I have taken someone's picture with this spoon. Who is it?" The partner will name the one the leader imitated.

17. **In Cahoots.** This trick is done the same as Spoon Photography, except as the person leaves the room the leader will ask, "Are you in cahoots?" meaning "Did you notice who was the last one to speak?" That person is the one.

18. **Danish Fish Game.** Players are seated in pairs on just enough chairs and each pair has a secret fish name such as carp or goldfish. One couple walks around the room calling off names of fish. As a couple's fish name is called they must leave their seats and follow the leading couple. After several pairs are following them, the leaders may say, "The ocean is stormy" and everyone must find a seat. One couple will be left to be the new leaders. If the leaders want everyone to leave their seats they say, "The ocean is calm."

19. **Flash Cards.** Make ahead of time 8½" x 11" flash cards of the letters of the alphabet. Divide your crowd into two or more teams. Display a letter and say, "Give me the name of a _____ that starts with the letter __." For categories use Christmas presents, Santa's reindeer, cities in the Holy Land, books of the Bible, birds, animals, trees, rivers, or most anything. The first person to fill in the answer receives the flash card. When you have used up all twenty-six letters the team that has the most cards wins.

20. **Old Plug.** Players stand in a circle around four others who put their arms around each other in a line to form a horse—Old Plug. The players try to hit Old Plug in the tail with a volleyball. When a player is successful he becomes the horse's head person; and the tail person takes a place in the circle, always using three to four persons as Old Plug.

21. **Crows and Cranes.** Players form two teams and line up fairly close to each other. Each team, Crows and Cranes, has a home line about ten to twenty feet away. The leader calls out, "Crrrrrr . . ." and finally calls one of the two names. That side must run while the others try to catch them. Anyone

who is caught must join the other team. The leader may mix the players up by calling, "Crackers," "Christmas," "Kraut," or some other word beginning with that sound.

22. **Table Hockey.** Form two teams, one on each side of a Ping-Pong table. Players try to blow a Ping-Pong ball off their opponents' side of the table. Set a top score for winning.

23. **Old Car Relay.** Teams of eight stand behind the starting line and each player is given an assignment. The goal should be about fifteen feet away. Player 1 has a flat tire, hops on right foot. Player 2 has a flat tire, hops on left foot. Player 3 can move only in reverse. Player 4 has water in gas, takes two steps forward and one step back. Player 5 has to be cranked every fourth step (cranks himself). Player 6 won't go at all, so Player 7 pushes him. Player 8 runs fine. The first team to finish wins.

Balloon Games

Use these at Christmas or any time, in socials for any age.

1. **Hot Air.** Give each person a balloon of the same size. On signal everyone blows to see who can reach the bursting point first. This game can be played in pairs with losers dropping out. Continue playing until you discover who has the most hot air.

2. **Balloon Sweep Relay.** Form two or more teams of five or six players. They are to stand in large circles. Give each team a blown-up balloon, a broom, and some spare balloons. On signal each first player takes the broom and sweeps the balloon around the circle and back to the second player, and so on. If the balloon is broken a member of the team must

blow up and tie another. The first team to sweep the balloon to each player wins.

3. **Balloon Volleyball.** Mark your own volleyball court with chalk on the floor. Tie up a string for the net. Set chairs up for each position. Players must stay seated except for rotating. The object is to knock the balloon so that it touches the floor in the opponent's territory. Regular volleyball rules are used.

4. **Balloon Basketball.** Two teams of five each sit in chairs in two lines facing each other, close enough that opponents' feet touch. "Goalies" sit in chairs at the head and foot of the two lines. Each team's goal is to the right. The goalie makes a hoop with his arms and may bend or contort in any way to let the balloon through for points, but he may not leave his chair.

The game is started by a referee tossing the balloon up in the middle of the two lines. A goal is two points. Each quarter is five minutes long.

5. **Balloon Battle.** Players form pairs for this game. One in in each pair has a balloon tied to his ankle. The partners join hands and step on other's balloons and try to defend their own. When a pair's balloon is broken they are finished.

6. **Balloon Relays.** Form two or more teams of equal size. Each contest starts on signal and the team to finish first wins.

Kick Relay. One at a time each player kicks a balloon to the goal—a line marked on the floor about fifteen feet away. Then he breaks the balloon by stomping on it, runs to touch the hand of the next player, and goes to the end of the line.

Batting Relay. Each person is given a cardboard bat. He must bat the balloon to the goal, break it by hugging it, then rush back to touch the next player.

Balloon Pass. Each team is given a small balloon. The first person puts the balloon under his chin and passes it to the next person who receives it under his chin, and so on.

The Christmas Stagecoach

A narrator tells this story while participants of all ages respond. It can be done with any seated group, around a campfire, in a fellowship hall or auditorium: even at a banquet.

1. Count off by sixes. The ones are the cowboys; twos are Indians; threes are women; fours are stagecoaches; fives are rifles; sixes are bows and arrows. All present are horses.

As the narration is read, each group gives a very loud, lively response when their names are mentioned. Cowboys yell "Hi! Hi!" as if urging on the horses of the stage. Indians stand and give a yell. Women scream at the top of their voices. Stagecoaches stand, turn completely around, and sit down. Rifles aim and fire, "Bang!" Bows and arrows draw bow and shout, "Zing!" for the flight of the arrow.

When horses are mentioned, everybody makes horse running noises with feet or on knees with hands.

The Narration

This is a story of the old West at Christmas time in the days of stage-coaches and cowboys and Indians!

(Name three well-known local males) _____, _____, and _____ were the three courageous cowboys.

They and two women, _____ and _____ (name two local females) were on a trip abroad a stagecoach.

The stagecoach was pulled by four handsome horses. The driver left Dodge City knowing that there could be trouble ahead! The passengers knew that the most dangerous section of the trip was Dead Man's Curve.

As the stagecoach neared this spot one could see that the women were a bit nervous and the cowboys were alert, readying their rifles for any attack. Even the horses seemed to sense that something might be wrong. They were right.

When the stagecoach was on the curve, without warning came the spine-tingling cry of the Indians! Mounted on their horses, they rode wildly toward the stagecoach, aiming their bows and arrows!

The cowboys took aim with their rifles and fired. The women screamed! The horses pranced nervously. The Indians shot their bows and arrows again and rode off into the west.

The women fainted! The cowboys fired one more volley from their rifles, just to keep things noisy. The stagecoach reeled and rocked as the horses raced ahead, and soon they were at Carson City, where they said to everybody: "Merrrrrry Christmas!"

A Visit from St. Nick

J. Neal Griffith, of Indiana, Pennsylvania, devised this parody on "The Night Before Christmas." Use it at banquets or any social situation where people are seated.

The narrator reads the material. When he comes to a number, he pauses and loudly calls it out. The person with that number reads the answer slip which has been handed him.

Type all twenty-seven answer slips double space, then cut the paper in such a way that the slips can be handed out individually.

PROGRAMS AND PARTIES FOR CHRISTMAS

Narrator reads

'Twas the night before Christmas when all through the house
Not a creature was stirring **(1) but the cook mixing
cookies!**

The stockings were hung by the chimney with care,
In hopes that St. Nicholas **(2) would darn all their holes!**

The children were nestled all snug in their beds,
While visions of sugar-plums **(3) made them drool in their
pillows!**

And mama in her 'kerchief, and I in my cap,
Had just settled our brains **(4) by visiting a psychiatrist!**

When out on the lawn there arose such a clatter
I sprang from my bed **(5) to tell them to pipe down!**

Away to the window I flew like a flash,
Tore open the shutters **(6) and threw them on the dying
fire!**

The moon, on the breast of the new-fallen snow
Gave the luster of mid-day **(7) on the bicycle we forgot to
put in!**

When, what to my wondering eyes should appear,
But a miniature sleigh **(8) with hydromatic drive!**

With a little old driver, so lively and quick,
I knew in a moment it **(9) was the Fuller Brush man!**

More rapid than eagles his coursers they came,
And he whistled and shouted **(10) and raised his blood
pressure!**

98

"Now, Dasher! now, Dancer! now Prancer and Vixen!
On Comet! on, Cupid! **(11) on, sauerkraut and weiners!**

To the top of the porch! to the top of the wall!
Now dash away! dash away! **(12) and a dash of tomato
catsup!**

As dry leaves that before the wild hurricane fly,
When they meet with an obstacle **(13) pile up in the
corner.**

So up to the housetop the coursers they flew,
With a sleigh full of toys **(14) and some bubble gum too!**

And then in a twinkling I heard on the roof
The prancing and pawing **(15) of a TV repairman.**

As I drew in my head and was turning around,
Down the chimney St. Nicholas came **(16) knocking six
bricks loose!**

He was dressed all in fur, from his head to his foot,
And his clothes were all tarnished **(17) and ready for the
cleaners.**

A bundle of toys he had flung on his back
And he looked like a peddler **(18) in the (local) grocery
emporium.**
(Note: Choose a well-known grocery, especially if the owner
is well-known in the group.)

His eyes—how they twinkled! his dimples,—how merry!
His cheeks were like roses **(19) but not so expensive!**

His droll little mouth was drawn up like a bow
And the beard of his chin **(20) needed trimming a little.**

The stump of a pipe he held tight in his teeth,
And the smoke it encircled his head **(21) like a cigarette wreath.**

He had a broad face and a round little belly,
That shook when he laughed **(22) like a television picture!**

He was chubby and plump, a right jolly old elf,
And I laughed when I saw him **(23) My wool underwear tickled me!**

A wink of his eye, and a twist of his head
Soon gave me to know **(24) he'd got a cinder in his eye!**

He spoke not a word, but went straight to his work,
And filled all the stockings **(25) but the ones with holes in them.**

He sprang to his sleigh, to his team gave a whistle,
And away they all flew **(26) they thought it was a cop.**

But I heard him exclaim, ere he drove out of sight,
"Happy Christmas to all" **(27) Aren't you glad this is over?**

Note: Change the responses if you like.

6

Christmas Prose and Poetry

A "Say and Do" Christmas Story
Alan T. Jones, Merom, Indiana

This story is to be memorized and given by a narrator. It is especially effective when used for young children, or groups containing young children. Candlelight or firelight is good to set the mood.

The storyteller gets the children to come up very close. Each person in the audience repeats line by line and gesture by gesture what the leader says and does. Explain . . . and practice.

In this story each listener pretends he is a shepherd boy on the hills outside Bethlehem. The sun has gone down and it is beginning to get dark. (Encourage everyone to participate).

Begin by singing the first stanza of "Silent Night."

Narration:

It's cold *(hugging yourself)* . . .
I'll break more sticks *(over the knee, pantomined)* . . .
Lay them on the coals *(action)* . . .
Blow *(as if blowing a fire)* . . .
Blow again *(do so)*.
It's catching! *(smile and nod)* . . .
Feels good *(warm hands)*.

Little lamb . . . come here *(patting leg to show lamb where to come)*.
You're shivering . . . I'll rub you *(rubbing action, as if rubbing lamb)*.
Turn your head *(hold lamb's head in both hands, turn it)* . . .

See that woman *(point)* riding on a donkey . . .
Isn't she beautiful . . . she's tired . . . So many travelers today . . . *(shaking head)*
I hope there's room . . . in the inn.

Dad! *(looking over left shoulder)*. You scared me! . . . What's this? Some meat for me to eat? . . . It's frozen stiff . . . I'll put it under my left arm *(do that)* pick up a stick *(reach down)* sharpen the point *(make motions as if sharpening point with knife)* stick it in the meat *(do so)* roast it over the fire *(act that out)*. It's getting done . . . *(watching it)* smells good *(sniffing it)* tastes good *(eating)*.

Dad . . . I feel sleepy . . . will you watch the sheep . . . while I take a little nap? Thank you. *(Rest head on hands)*.

(Wakes suddenly!) What's that *(rubbing eyes)*. The brightest star . . . I've ever seen . . .
Listen *(cocking head)*. Someone is speaking! . . . "Unto you is born . . . in the city of David . . . a Savior" . . . Angels are singing . . . "Glory to God . . . in the highest . . . and on earth Peace . . . Good will to men."

Dad, let's go to Bethlehem. Let's run! *(clapping hands together in side-sweeping motion to imitate sound of running.)*
I'm out of breath *(panting)*. Look! *(pointing.)*
There's a light . . . in the barn . . . Let's knock *(knocks gently)*.
Shhh! . . . Baby's asleep *(in a whisper)*.

Look! In the hay . . . by the donkey . . .

He came . . . of Mary mild . . . to lead . . . God's whole creation . . . on peace . . . a little child!

Now sing softly the first stanza of "Away in a Manger."

Why the Chimes Rang
Raymond MacDonald Alden

This classic Christmas story to be read aloud is included with the awareness, that this is a day in which people do not hear many stories read or told. It could be used at a banquet, at the end of a party, or as a part of a Christmas program or message. Its simple eloquence is timeless, and expresses well the essence of the Christmas spirit.

There was once, in a far away country where few people have ever traveled, a wonderful church.

It stood high on a hill in the midst of a great city; and every Sunday, as well as on sacred days like Christmas, thousands of people climbed the hill to its great archways, looking like lines of ants all moving in the same direction.

When one came to the building itself, he found stone columns and dark passages, and a grand entrance leading to the main room of the church. This room was so long that one standing at the doorway could scarcely see the other end where the choir stood by the marble altar.

In the farthest corner was the organ; and this organ was so loud that, sometimes when it played, the people for miles around would close their shutters and prepare for a great thunderstorm!

Altogether, no such church as this was ever seen before, especially when it was lighted up for some festival and crowded with people, young and old. But the strangest thing about the whole building was the wonderful chime of bells.

At the one corner of the church was a great gray tower with ivy growing over it as far up as one could see. I say as far as one could see, because the tower was quite great enough to fit the great church, and it rose so far into the sky that it was only in very fair weather that anyone claimed to be able to see the top. Even then one could not be certain that it was in sight. Up and up and up climbed the stones and the ivy; and, as the men who built the church had been dead for hundreds of years, everyone had forgotten how high the tower was supposed to be.

Now all the people knew that at the top of the tower was a chime of Christmas bells.

They had hung there ever since the church had been built and were the most beautiful bells in the world. Some thought it was because a great musician had cast them and arranged them in their place; others said it was because of the great height, which reached up where the air was clearest and purest. However that might be, no one who had ever heard the chimes denied that they were the sweetest in the world. Some described them as sounding like angels far up in the sky; others like strange winds singing through the trees.

But the fact was that no one had heard them for years and years. There was an old man, living not far from the church, who said that his mother had spoken of hearing them when she was a little girl, and he was the only one who was sure of as much as that.

They were Christmas chimes, you see, and were not meant to be played by men or on common days.

It was the custom on Christmas Eve for all the people to bring to the church their offerings to the Christ child; and when the greatest and best offering was laid on the altar, there used to come sounding through the music of the choir the Christmas chimes far up in the tower.

Some said that the wind rang them; others that they were so high that the angels could set them swinging. But for many long years they had never been heard. It is said that people had been growing less careful of their gifts for the Christ child, and that no offering was brought great enough to deserve the music of the chimes.

Every Christmas Eve the rich people still crowded to the altar, each one trying to bring some better gift than any other, without giving anything that he wanted for himself, and the church was crowded with those who thought that perhaps the wonderful bells might be heard again.

But although the service was splendid and the offerings plenty, only the roar of the wind could be heard far up in the stone tower.

Now, a number of miles from the city in a little country village, where nothing could be seen of the great church but glimpses of the tower when the weather was fine, lived a boy named Pedro and his little brother.

They knew very little about the Christmas chimes, but they had heard of the service in the church on Christmas Eve, and had a secret plan, which they had often talked over when by themselves, to go to see the beautiful celebration.

"Nobody can guess, Little Brother," Pedro would say, "all the fine things there are to see and hear; and I have even heard it said that the Christ child sometimes comes down to bless the service. What if we could see *Him*?"

The day before Christmas was bitterly cold, with a few lonely snowflakes flying in the air and a hard, white crust on the ground. Sure enough, Pedro and Little Brother were able to slip quietly away early in the afternoon; and although the walking was hard in the frosty air, before nightfall they had trudged so far, hand in hand, that they saw the lights of the big city just ahead of them.

Indeed, they were about to enter one of the great gates in the wall that surrounded it, when they saw something dark on the snow near their path and stepped aside to look at it.

It was a poor woman who had fallen just outside the city, too sick and tired to get in where she might have found shelter. The soft snow made of a drift a sort of pillow for her, and she would soon be so sound asleep in the wintry air that no one could ever waken her again.

All this Pedro saw in a moment, and he knelt down beside her and tried to rouse her, even tugging at her arm a little, as though he would have tried to carry her away.

He turned her face toward him so that he could rub some of the snow on it, and when he had looked at her silently a moment, he stood up again and said; "It's no use, Little Brother. You will have to go on alone."

"Alone?" cried Little Brother. "And you not see the Christmas festival?"

"No," said Pedro, and he could not keep back a bit of choking sound in his throat. "See this poor woman. Her face looks like the Madonna in the chapel window, and she will freeze to death if nobody cares for her. Everyone has gone to the church now, and when you come back you can bring some-one to help her. I will rub her to keep her from freezing, and perhaps get her to eat the bun that is left in my pocket."

"But I cannot bear to leave you and go on alone," said Little Brother.

"Both of us need not miss the service," said Pedro, "and it is better I than you. You can easily find your way to the church. You must see and hear everything twice, Little Brother—once for you and once for me. I am sure the Christ child must know how I should love to come with you and worship Him. And, oh, if you get a chance, Little Brother, to slip up to the altar without getting in anyone's way, take this little silver piece of mine and lay it down for my offering when no one is looking.

"Do not forget where you have left me. Forgive me for not going with you."

In this way he hurried Little Brother off to the city and winked hard to keep back the tears as he heard the crunching footsteps sounding farther and farther away in the twilight. It was pretty hard to lose the music and splendor of the Christmas celebration that he had been planning for so long and spend the time instead in that lonely place in the snow.

The great church was a wonderful place that night. Everyone said that it had never looked so bright and beautiful before! When the organ played and the thousands of people sang, the walls shook with the sound, and little Pedro, away outside the city wall, felt the earth tremble around him!

At the close of the service came the procession with the offerings to be laid on the altar. Rich men and great men marched proudly up to lay down their gifts for the Christ child.

Some brought wonderful jewels, some baskets of gold so heavy they could scarcely carry them down the aisle!

A great writer laid down a book that he had been making for years and years. And last of all walked the king of the country, hoping with all the rest to win for himself the chime of the Christmas bells. There went a great murmur through the church as the people saw the king take from his head the royal crown, all set with precious stones, and lay it gleaming on the altar, as his offering to the Holy Child.

"Surely," everyone said, "we shall hear the bells now, for nothing like this has ever happened before!"

But still only the cold wind was heard in the tower, and the people shook their heads. Some of them said, as they had before, that they never really believed the story of the chimes and doubted if they ever rang at all.

The procession was over, and the choir began the closing hymn.

Suddenly the organist stopped playing as though he had been shot. Everyone looked at the old minister, standing by the altar, holding up his hand for silence.

Not a sound could be heard from anyone in the church, but as all the people strained to listen, there came softly but distinctly, swinging through the air, *the sound of the chimes in the tower!*

So far away, and yet so clear the music seemed—so much sweeter were the notes than anything that had been heard before, rising and falling away up there in the sky, that the people in the church sat for a moment as still as though something held each of them by the shoulders. Then they all stood up together and stared straight at the altar, to see what great gift had awakened the long-silent bells.

But all that the nearest of them saw was the childish figure of Little Brother, who had crept softly down the aisle when few were looking, and had laid Pedro's little piece of silver on the altar!

One Solitary Life

He was born in an obscure village, the child of a peasant woman. He grew up in still another village, where he worked in a carpenter shop until he was thirty. Then for three years he was an itinerant preacher. He never wrote a book. He never held an office. He never had a family or owned a house. He didn't go to college. He never visited a big city. He never traveled two hundred miles from the place where he was born. He did none of the things one usually associates with greatness. He had no credentials but himself. He was only thirty-three when the tide of public opinion turned against him. His friends ran away. He was turned over to his enemies and went through the mockery of a trial. He was nailed to a cross between two thieves. While he was dying, his executioners gambled for his clothing, the only property he had on earth. When he was dead, he was laid in a borrowed grave through the pity of a friend. Nineteen centuries have come and gone, and today he is the central figure of the human race and the leader of mankind's progress. All the armies that ever marched, all the navies that ever sailed, all the parliaments that ever sat, all the kings that ever reigned, put together, have not affected the life of man on this earth as much as that One Solitary Life.

James A. Francis, D.D.

Is There a Santa Claus?

This editorial first appeared in the *New York Sun* on September 21, 1897:

We take pleasure in answering at once the communication below, expressing at the same time our great gratification that its faithful author is numbered among the friends of *The Sun*.

Dear Editor:

I am eight years old.

Some of my little friends say there is no Santa Claus.

Papa says, "If you see it in *The Sun* it's so." Please tell me the truth. Is there a Santa Claus?

Virginia O'Hanlon
115 W. 95th Street

Virginia, your little friends are wrong!

They have been affected by the skepticism of a skeptical age.

They do not believe except what they see. They think that nothing can be which is not comprehensible by their little minds.

All minds, Virginia, whether they be men's or children's are little. In this great universe of ours man is a mere insect, an ant, in his intellect, as compared with the boundless world about him, as measured by the intelligence capable of grasping the whole truth and knowledge.

Yes, Virginia, there is a Santa Claus. He exists as certainly as love and generosity and devotion exist, and you know that they abound and give to your life its highest beauty and joy.

Alas! How dreary would be the world if there were no Santa Claus! It would be as dreary as if there were no Virginias.

There would be no childlike faith then—no poetry, no romance to make tolerable this existence. We should have no enjoyment except in sense and sight. The eternal light with which childhood fills the world would be extinguished.

Not believe in Santa Claus! You might as well not believe in fairies! You might get your papa to hire men to watch in all the chimneys on Christmas Eve to catch Santa Claus, but even if they did not see Santa Claus coming down, what would that prove?

Nobody sees Santa Claus, but that is no sign that there is no Santa Claus. The most real things in the world are those that neither children nor men can see. Did you ever see fairies dancing on the lawn? Of course not, but that's no proof that they are not there.

Nobody can conceive or imagine all the wonders there are unseen and unseeable in the world.

You tear apart a baby's rattle and see what makes the noise inside, but there is a veil covering the unseen world which not the strongest man, nor even the united strength of all the strongest men that ever lived, could tear apart.

Only faith, fancy, poetry, love, romance can push aside that curtain and view and picture the supernal beauty and glory beyond. Is it all real? Ah, Virginia, in all this world there is nothing else real and abiding.

No Santa Claus? Thank God, he lives, and he lives forever. A thousand years from now, Virginia—nay, ten times ten thousand years from now, he will continue to make glad the heart of childhood.

What Can I Give Him?

What can I give Him, poor as I am?
If I were a shepherd, I would bring a lamb,
If I were a Wise Man, I would do my part—
    Yet what I can, I give him,
  Give my heart!

—Christina G. Rossetti

111

I Heard the Bells on Christmas Day

I heard the bells on Christmas Day,
   Their old familiar carols play,
And wild and sweet the words repeat
   Of "peace on earth, good will to men!"

I thought how, as the day had come,
   The belfries of all Christendom
Had rolled along the unbroken song
   Of "peace on earth, good will to men!"

And in despair I bowed by head;
   "There is no 'peace on earth,' " I said;
"For hate is strong and mocks the song
   Of 'peace on earth, good will to men' "

Then pealed the bells, more loud and deep—
   God is not dead, nor does He sleep!
The wrong shall fail, the right prevail
   With "peace on earth, good will to men!"

And so my heart was lifted high,
   My eyes and thoughts looked to the sky,
And once again, I heard it then,
   Yes, "Peace on earth, good will to men!"
                Henry W. Longfellow

Keep Christ In Christmas

As now we celebrate His birth—
The coming of the Christ to earth—
May we amid our joyous mirth
   Keep Jesus first in Christmas.

As chiming bells ring out their lay
And hearts are merry, light and gay
Remember it is His birthday—
   Keep Jesus first in Christmas!

We sing of Him in carols sweet,
We lay our best gifts at His feet,
This way is Christmas joy complete—
   With Jesus first in Christmas!

Selected

Too Small

"Father, where shall I work today?"
And my love flowed warm and free.
Then He pointed me to a tiny spot
And said, "Tend that for Me."

I answered quickly, "Oh, no, not that.
Why no one would ever see
No matter how well my work was done—
No, not that place for me!"

The word that He spoke He spoke in love,
He answered me tenderly,
"Ah, little one, search the heart of yours,
Are you working for them or Me?
Bethlehem too was a small, little place
And so was Galilee!"

Sunday School Times

In a Child

An Angel paused in his downward flight
   With a seed of truth and love and light;

113

And he said, "Where must this seed be sown
  To bring most fruit when it is grown?"

The Lord responded; He said and smiled,
"Go plant it for Me in the heart of a child!"

What Each Did

In a rude stable cold
The friendly beasts their stories told:

"I," said the donkey, shaggy and brown,
"Carried his mother up hill and down,
Carried her safe to Bethlehem town."

"I," said the cow, all white and red,
"Gave Him my manger for His bed,
Gave Him my hay to pillow His head."

"I," said the sheep, with the curly horn,
"Gave Him wool for His blanket warm;
He wore my coat on Christmas morn."

"I," said the camel, all yellow and black,
"Over the desert, upon my back,
Brought Him gifts in the Wise Men's pack."

"I," said the dove, "from my rafter high,
Cooed Him to sleep that He should not cry!
We cooed Him to sleep, my mate and I."

So every beast, by some good spell
In the stable darkness was able to tell
Of the gift he gave to Emmanuel!

Robert Davis

Openness

My latch is on the string tonight,
  The hearth fire is aglow
I seem to hear swift passing feet—
  The Christ child in the snow.

My heart is open wide tonight
  For stranger, kith or kin,
I would not close a single door
  Where Christ may enter in!

                              Anonymous

A Glad New Year

Ah, dearest, Jesus, Holy child,
  Make Thee a bed, soft, undefiled
Within my heart, that it may be
  A quiet chamber, kept for Thee.

My heart for very joy does leap
  My lips no more can silence keep,
I too must sing with joyful tongue
  That sweetest ancient cradle song.

Glory to God in highest Heaven,
  Who unto man His Son has given,
While angels sing with pious mirth
  A glad New Year to all the earth!

                              Martin Luther

If Christ Had not Come

If Christ had not been born,
Hearts burdened and forlorn

Must seek in vain
Peace to attain,
If Christ had not been born.

If to the Bethlehem home
The Christ child had not come,
Hearts now agleam
With love would seem
Drear, had not Christ come.

But now both hope and cheer
God gives for every year;
To seeking hearts
His grace imparts
His love, for Christ has come!

Fred Shephard

What Christmas Is

What is the thought of Christmas? Giving.
What is the hope of Christmas? Living.
What is the joy of Christmas? Love.
No silver or gold is needed for giving
If the heart is filled with Christmas love,
For the hope of the world is kindly living,
Learned from the joy of God above.

Laura Hooker

The Innkeeper

I only did what you have done
A thousand times or more,

When Joseph came to Bethlehem
  And knocked upon my door.
I did not turn the Christ away
  With alibi so deft.
Like you, I simply gave to him
  Whatever I had left!
                    Gordon Pratt Baker

My Christmas Prayer

God grant these gifts to you—
His star to lead you on your way,
The joy, the faith, the friendship
That comes with this glad day,
And ever in the New Year
Like an answer to a prayer,
The light of peace to bless you
And guide you—everywhere.
                    Anonymous

A Christmas Creed

I *believe* in Jesus Christ and in the beauty of the gospel that
  began in Bethlehem.
I *believe* in Him whom the kings of the earth ignored,
  and the proud can never understand,
  Whose path was among the common people,
  Whose welcome came from men of hungry hearts.
I *believe in Him* who proclaimed the love of God to be
  invincible,
  Whose cradle was a mother's arms,

117

Whose home in Nazareth had love for its only wealth,
Who looked at men and made them see what His love
saw in them,
Who by his love brought sinners back to purity
And lifted human weakness up to meet the strength of
God.
I *confess* my everlasting need of God: the need of forgiveness
for my greed and selfishness,
The need of life for empty soul,
The need of warmth for heart grown cold.
I *acknowledge* the glory of all that is like Christ:
The steadfastness of friends,
The blessedness of home,
The beauty of compassion,
The courage of those who dare to resist all passion and
hate.
I *believe* that only by love expressed shall the earth at length
be purified,
And I acknowledge in Christ
A faith that sees beyond our present evil,
And I pray that this redemption may begin in me now in
this Christmas season as I pray.

Walter Russell Bowie

The Night Before Christmas

'Twas the night before Christmas when all through the house
Not a creature was stirring, not even a mouse;
The stockings were hung by the chimney with care,
In hopes that St. Nicholas soon would be there;
The children were nestled all snug in their beds,
While visions of sugar-plums danced in their heads;

And mama in her 'kerchief, and I in my cap,
Had just settled our brains for a long winter's nap,
When out on the lawn there arose such a clatter,
I sprang from my bed to see what was the matter.
Away to the window I flew like a flash,
Tore open the shutters and threw up the sash.
The moon on the breast of the new-fallen snow
Gave the lustre of mid-day to objects below,
When, what to my wondering eyes should appear,
But a miniature sleigh, and eight tiny reindeer,
With a little old driver, so lively and quick,
I knew in a moment it must be St. Nick.
More rapid than eagles his coursers they came,
And he whistled, and shouted, and called them by name;
"Now, Dasher! now, Dancer! now, Prancer and Vixen!
On, Comet! on Cupid! on, Donder and Blitzen!
To the top of the porch! to the top of the wall!
Now dash away! dash away! dash away all!"
As dry leaves that before the wild hurricane fly,
When they meet with an obstacle, mount to the sky,
So up to the house-top the coursers they flew,
With the sleigh full of toys, and St. Nicholas too.
And then, in a twinkling, I heard on the roof
The prancing and pawing of each little hoof.
As I drew in my head, and was turning around,
Down the chimney St. Nicholas came with a bound.
He was dressed all in fur, from his head to his foot,
And his clothes were all tarnished with ashes and soot;
A bundle of toys he had flung on his back.
And he looked like a peddler just opening his pack.
His eyes—how they twinkled! his dimples how merry!
His cheeks were like roses, his nose like a cherry!
His droll little mouth was drawn up like a bow,

119

And the beard of his chin was as white as the snow;
The stump of a pipe he held tight in his teeth,
And the smoke it encircled his head like a wreath;
He had a broad face and a little round belly,
That shook, when he laughed, like a bowlful of jelly.
He was chubby and plump, a right jolly old elf,
And I laughed when I saw him, in spite of myself;
A wink of his eye and a twist of his head,
Soon gave me to know I had nothing to dread;
He spoke not a word, but went straight to his work,
And filled all the stockings; then turned with a jerk,
And laying his finger aside of his nose,
And giving a nod, up the chimney he rose;
He sprang to his sleigh, to his team gave a whistle,
And away they flew like the down of a thistle.
But I heard him exclaim, ere he drove out of sight,
"Happy Christmas to all, and to all a good-night."

Clement Clarke Moore